TUG HILL COUNTRY
COUNTRY

Tales from the Big Woods

Harold E. Samson

NORTH COUNTRY BOOKS
Utica, New York

TUG HILL COUNTRY

Tales from the Big Woods

Manufactured by Canterbury Press
Rome, NY

ISBN 978-0-925168-84-9

First Printing — May 1971
Second Printing — August 1971
Third Printing — February 1972
Fourth Printing — January 1974
Fifth Printing — June 1975
Sixth Printing — December 1982
First Paperback Printing — June 2002

NORTH COUNTRY BOOKS
311 Turner Street
Utica, New York 13501

*Dedicated to my mother and
father, Ida and Edward Samson,
who laid the foundations
for a good life.*

ACKNOWLEDGMENTS

The author hereby thanks the following periodicals and publications for pertinent information derived from perusal of their files and pages: Everett's History of Oswego County, Hough's History of Jefferson County, History of the Town of Orwell, Jefferson County Gazeteer, History of the Town of Sandy Creek, The Pulaski Democrat, The Sandy Creek News, the Watertown Daily Times, The Oswego Palladium-Times, The Lumber Camp News, and The Northeastern Logger.

Special thanks also go to Miss Nanette Hamer, Sandy Creek Town Historian, for the use of voluminous notes and clippings; to John Hogan, for his invaluable knowledge of Tug Hill lumbering; to Rev. Frank A. Reed, for his valued advice and interest, and the loan of many pictures and sources of information; to Percy Caster, also for the use of various photos used herein; and to Rev. John Crandall for notes on the Greenfield case.

Also, special belated thanks to Thomas W. Hamer and Wilbur W. Wilcox, both deceased, for their many reminiscences and the encouragement that they offered.

INTRODUCTION

A word of explanation to acquaint the reader with just what constitutes Tug Hill Country having been deemed advisable, the writer has hereby set himself to accomplish this purpose. But he has quickly found that what at first seemed to be a short and easy chore, has suddenly become a complex and difficult task.

To begin with, Tug Hill is not actually a hill at all, at least not a hill that one may climb, and resting on the crest, say to oneself, "I have reached the top." Far from it.

Instead, Tug Hill is a region, a vast territory, a conglomerate jumble of rugged slopes and gullies, heavily wooded in most places but rocky and barren in others, that were thrown together at some remote time and by some terrific upheaval to form a gigantic plateau covering many square miles.

Again, the word "plateau" is not truly descriptive. A true plateau has a flat or level area on its top. Tug Hill does not. Its crest is cut by as many creeks and gorges and little valleys as are its sides. A hiker starting at any given point at its base and traveling straight up over its top, never knows for sure just when he has reached that top. His first indication that he has done so is when, suddenly, the little streams that he encounters flow in the opposite direction.

The roads that lead into and through the area, with very few exceptions, are narrow and twisting, following the easiest grades, many of them of the gravel variety. They are not good roads, as judged by present-day standards. The better roads are mostly confined to the edges, especially along the eastern and southern slopes, where lie a few excellent but rolling farming areas. Many of the little valleys have rich and productive soil, but the altitude is high and the growing seasons are short.

Tug Hill is, and always has been, noted for its winter snows. Some mysterious thermal funnel from off the eastern end of Lake Ontario brings to the region a wealth of moisture-laden winds. These air currents, rising high above the upsweeping western end of the escarpment, bring plentiful rainfall in summer and blinding blizzards in winter; blizzards that sometimes last for days and deposit prodigious depths of snow.

Sears Pond and Highmarket, both situated at about the highest points on the plateau, have the dubious distinction of being the recipients of the greatest annual falls of snow of any place in the state, if not the whole eastern seaboard.

At least one business enterprise has capitalized on this natural phenomenon. Snow Ridge, situated near Turin on the northeast slope, has become one of the most successful ski resorts of New York State.

In winter, the Tug Hill plateau becomes a vast wilderness of white; favorite playground of snowmobilers and other winter sports enthusiasts. In spring and summer, it takes on a mantel of green that transforms it into a veritable paradise for the nature lover. In fall it is a riot of flaming reds and golds that attract sightseers from far and near, as well as hundreds of Nimrods who come to pursue the crafty deer and bear.

This is Tug Hill. Tug Hill Country is all this and much, much more.

Tug Hill Country embraces not only the plateau itself, but all the vast regions that are watered by and drained by the tumultous streams that come down from its flinty slopes, and through its rocky gorges.

Its tremendous watershed and thousands of springs give birth to many famous streams. The mighty Mohawk utters its first infant gurglings high up near the crest of the Hill, and fed by the springs of the area, made tough and arrogant by the gigantic yearly runoff of snow water, it dashes down through West Leyden on the south face, and at last into its own basin for its journey to join the Hudson.

Salmon River, Mad River, and Deer River all find their beginnings in the same manner and in the same general region, but these make their boisterous journeys down the west and north slopes. Roaring Brook, Fish Creek, Cottrell Creek, The Raystone, and Big and Little Sandy Creeks all have their initial being among the snows and rocky forests of the plateau and go their separate ways; sometimes close together but always individual and apart.

Even Black River, while not dependent upon the area for its origins, benefits mightily from its drainage as it curves around the base of the Hill for many miles.

Tug Hill Country is not just a hill, or a jumble of hills, or a region. It is also forest solitudes, and wild beasts, and tumbling trout streams that were once sources of unlimited water power. It is lumber camps and backwoods farms and high, stony pastures. It is desolation in winter and breathtaking beauty at all other times of the year. It is wild flowers and bird song and the music of winds in the evergreens. It is humor and tragedy, courage and high resolve, success and failure. It is legend and fact, folklore and reality. It is self-reliance and ingenuity, and the will to survive. It is patriotism and mother-love, pride and honor, memory of the past and trust in the future.

It is America.

TABLE OF CONTENTS

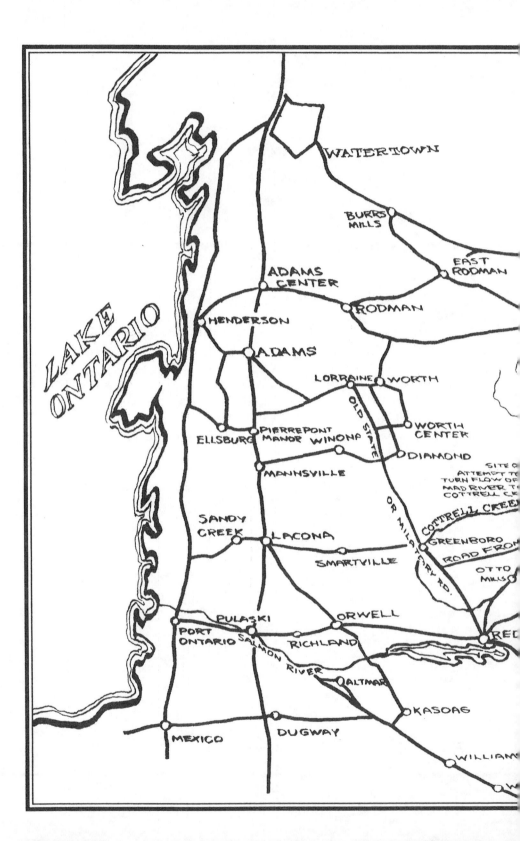

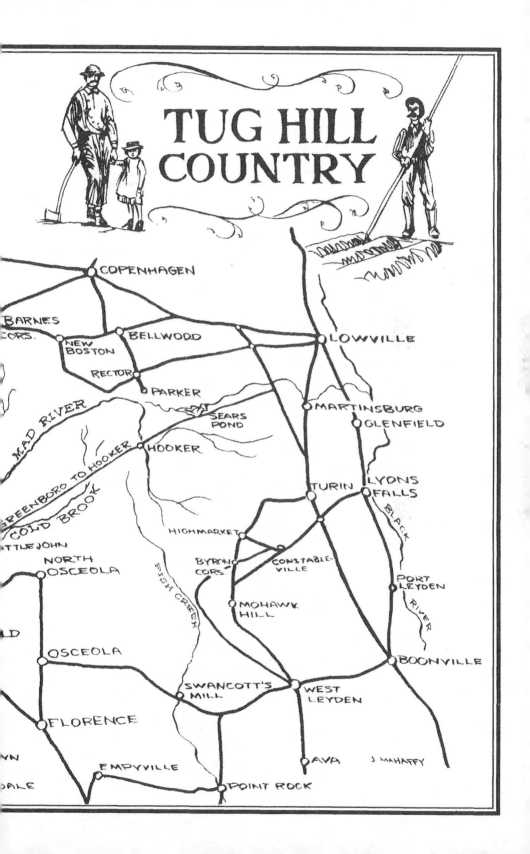

TUG HILL COUNTRY

COPENHAGEN

BARNES CORS.

NEW BOSTON

BELLWOOD

RECTOR

PARKER

LOWVILLE

MARTINSBURG

GLENFIELD

MAD RIVER

SEARS POND

GREENBORO TO HOOKER

HOOKER

COLD BROOK

LITTLEJOHN

NORTH OSCEOLA

HIGHMARKET

TURIN

LYONS FALLS

BLACK

BYRON CORS.

CONSTABLE-VILLE

MOHAWK HILL

PORT LEYDEN

RIVER

FISH CREEK

OSCEOLA

BOONVILLE

FLORENCE

SWANCOTT'S MILL

WEST LEYDEN

EMPYVILLE

POINT ROCK

AVA

J. MAHAFFY

DALE

ILLUSTRATIONS

COLONEL MEACHAM'S
BIG CHEESE

Among the first pioneers to invade the wilderness that was later to become the Town of Sandy Creek, in northwestern Oswego County, were two brothers named John and Simon Meacham. In the year of 1806 these two, accompanied by Ephriam Brewster, arrived and purchased lands in what is now the southern end of the town, where they built their cabins and set about the task of clearing farms.

Here in the wilderness, the daughter of one of these Meacham families evidently discovered her life-mate, as the first marriage in this territory is recorded as having taken place that same year between Lucy Meacham and Henry Patterson.

Later in the year, Simon enlarged his house and equipped it to serve as a tavern; this constituting the first hostelry in the locality. During the next year, 1807, he expanded still further by stocking his place with trade goods and turning it into the town's first store.

For the next few years, during which time the whole of northern New York flamed with the savage fury of the War of 1812, the Meacham interests continued to expand and prosper. Twice during the troubled year of 1813, Captain John Meacham raised a company of militia and led them on forced marches to Sackets Harbor, where attacks by the British fleet were believed immi-

1

nent. But both times the attacks failed to materialize, and the troops marched home again without firing a shot.

By the time the citizens of the territory decided to hold their first town meeting, in May of 1825, Simon Meacham had become one of the most influential men for miles around, and was elected to serve as the first supervisor of the newly formed township of Washington-ville, later Sandy Creek.

Some time prior to this, the first two Meachams had been joined by another and younger brother, Colonel Thomas S. Meacham. He also purchased land and settled in the southern part of the town, on what was then called the Old Salt Road, but now known as U.S. Route 11. Here he settled down to the serious business of agriculture.

Arriving as he did at a much later date than his brothers, Colonel Meacham could add but little to the impressive list of "firsts" which had been established by them. But he determined to make up with other superlatives what he lacked in this respect. The home and farm buildings that he erected on his properties were among the most pretentious and extensive in the township, and the dairy which he built up became by far the largest. The milk from this dairy was converted into cheese in his own factory, along with that furnished by neighboring farmers.

Early in the year of 1835, Colonel Meacham's active mind began to toy with an idea which he believed might bring fame to both himself and the town in which he lived. Somewhere he had heard that President Andrew Jackson had a great fondness for good cheese. Why not send him a cheese . . . a special cheese made expressly for him?

From this point on, the grandiose in the colonel's

2

soul took complete control of his reasoning. It would have to be an exceedingly large cheese, large enough to demand attention. Why not the most mammoth that the state had ever produced? Why not, indeed, the largest in the nation . . . the world?

The more the colonel thought about the idea, the more it appealed to him. After a great deal of figuring, he desided that a cheese weighing one thousand pounds would do the trick. A half-ton of solid cheese! What a stupendous idea . . . what a stupendous task!

By September the colonel's plans had reached completion, and preparation for their fulfillment began. Of course his cheese factory was not equipped to turn out a product of such gigantic proportions, so he hired carpenters to build a special structure, containing a frame, hoops, and press several feet in diameter. The frame was lined with special cheese-cloth of exceedingly heavy quality.

For five days the curd made from the milk of the colonel's 150 cow dairy was piled into this frame. Each day the press was brought into use and the whey was carefully squeezed out. At the end of the five days, the cheese had reached the approximate weight originally planned, but still it did not satisfy the colonel. So two more day's curd was added, at the end of which time the weight of the product had grown to 1,400 pounds.

This, the colonel decided, should suffice, and he ordered the cheese boxed and sealed. The next item in the order of business now was the delivery of the monster to President Jackson in Washington.

This in itself was no mean task in that day and age, and entailed a great deal of careful planning. Always a believer in the value of the spectacular, Colonel

3

Meacham reasoned that the delivery must be as unusual as was the cheese itself.

With this in mind he selected a large and sturdy wagon which he had brightly painted, and into this the gigantic cheese was loaded. For motive power, the colonel had decided upon a team of forty-eight gray horses; not because it actually required so many, but because such a number would add greatly to the show. Of course he did not have that many of his own, so he searched the surrounding region for a source of supply. Every matched gray team that he discovered was hired to join the cavalcade, along with its owner as driver.

When twenty-four such teams had been found, they were assembled at the Meacham farm, where they were groomed and polished, and their harnesses were decorated with brightly hued rings and roseattes. Then one morning they were all hitched to the resplendent wagon, and the big cheese rolled out on the first leg of its trip to Washington.

Colorful indeed was the procession which set out from the Meacham farm on that memorable morning. The wagon had been festooned and decorated with bright flags and streamers, and the spokes of its wheels interwoven with strips of bunting which turned them into rolling kaleidoscopes of color. Out in front, the forty-eight gray horses in their polished harness and gay decorations seemed to sense the festivity of the occasion and pranced their prettiest.

The cheese itself was protected from sun and weather by a covering of snowy cloth; and around its girth was fastened what was described by a witness as "a mighty national belt, colorfully representing the states, and bearing the motto 'The Union . . . It Must Be Preserved'."

Behind the wagon stretched a parade nearly a mile

4

in length, made up of neighboring farmers and their families who had been invited by the colonel to go along on the rtip to Port Ontario. These folks were dressed in their Sunday best and driving their finest rigs, and contributed much to the holiday aspect of the affair.

A stop was made at the village of Pulaski to allow the people to gaze in awe at the world's largest cheese, after which the entourage resumed its journey to The Port, arriving there that afternoon. One can only imagine the furor caused by its advent into the little lakeside community, or the festivities that reigned there that night.

The next day, November 15th, the monster cheese was loaded onto a sailing vessel and started upon the water phase of its journey. As the boat left the dock, a band played and a cannon boomed in a salute to the colonel, who stood, a proud figure of a man, gaily waving from the deck.

The journey was accomplished by way of Lake Ontario to Oswego, and from there through the Oswego and Erie Canals; pausing at Syracuse, Rome, Utica, and Albany where the cheese was unveiled to the admiring view of the populace. Thus it was that long before the vessel sailed into the Potomac, the fame of Colonel Meacham and the magnificent gift which he was bringing to President Jackson had reached Washington.

Displaying a talent for flowery oratory fully equal to his other achievements, Colonel Meacham before a vast throng, presented the cheese to the President "with the compliments of the people of the State of New York and the Town of Sandy Creek." Old Hickory accepted with grace, although he must have secretly wondered what in the world he would ever do with so much cheese, and presented the colonel with half a dozen bottles of choice wine.

It was not until February 22, 1836, that the final chapter in the story of the big cheese was written. This day President Jackson designated as "cheese day," and on it he had the stupendous gift carved into small pieces, wrapped, and passed out to the populace of Washington. An eye-witness account of this event, published in a Washington newspaper, presented the following amusing picture to the public:

"This was Washington's Birthday; and the President, the departments, the Senate, and we the people, have celebrated by eating the Big Cheese. The President's house was thrown open, the multitude swarmed in. The Senate of the United States adjourned. The representatives of the various departments turned out. Representatives in swarms left the Capitol . . . all for the purpose of eating cheese. Mr. Webster was here to eat cheese. Mr. Woodbury, Mr. Dickerson, Colonel Benton, and the gallant Colonel Trobridge were eating cheese. The court, the fashion, the beauty of Washington, were all eating cheese. Officers in Washington, foreign representatives in stars and garters; gay, gorgeous, joyous and dashing women, in all the pride and panoply and pomp of wealth, were there eating cheese. Cheese . . . cheese . . . cheese . . . was on everybody's lips and in everybody's mouth. All you heard was cheese. All you saw was cheese. All you smelt was cheese. It was cheese; cheese; cheese. Streams of cheese were going up the avenue in everybody's fists. Balls of cheese were in hundreds of pockets. Every handkerchief smelt of cheese. The whole atmosphere for half a mile around was infected and reeked of cheese."

This subtle brand of ridicule by the Washington newspapers was somewhat alleviated by the receipt of a special citation from Governor Marcy of New York State, lauding the colonel for his outstanding achievements in attracting the attention of the nation to the agricultural products of the state.

According to old account books kept by the colonel and found many years later, the cost of making and delivering the Jackson cheese ran in the neighborhood of twelve hundred dollars. While this does not constitute a staggering sum in this day and age, in 1835 it was considered quite an amount for a farmer, even a very prosperous one, to spend in furthering the interests of his state and township.

In spite of the inevitable crop of uncomplimentary comment voiced by a few disgruntled individuals who rather envied him his notoriety, Colonel Meacham did not desist in his pursuit of superlatives. Four more large cheeses, each of seven hundred pounds weight, were manufactured and delivered to Vice-President Van Buren, Governor Marcy, and the mayors of New York City and Rochester.

The Rochester cheese was carved and packaged, and sold by the city government for the current price of fourteen cents a pound, the proceeds being used as the foundation of a Volunteer Firemen's Relief Fund. At the time of the last recorded information on the subject in 1911, this fund had grown to the sum of $80,000.

The Rochester mayor sent back to Colonel Meacham a large barrel of flour, equal in size to ten regular barrels, and weighing nearly a ton.

Soon after this the colonel turned his attention and never-flagging energies to a new project which he felt would be of vast benefit to the community. This was the erection on his farm of what was named the Agricultural Hall, designed with the intention of holding in it various fairs and expositions which he hoped would stimulate interest in advanced agricultural methods in the town. These hoped-for results did not materialize, and the building was used very little for these purposes.

The Hall was a large, rambling, two-story building, into the front of which he caused to be built one of his most prized possessions: the head of the immense flour barrel sent to him by the mayor of Rochester.

Reflecting his flair for the spectacular, on the roof was a large cupola, inside which revolved a life-sized wooden soldier, upraised sword in hand. This figure was kept in motion by an intricate system of ropes, weights, and pulleys.

The building endured until long after the death of its builder; part of it being moved years later to a higher location nearby, where it was converted into a farmhouse that still stands today.

Colonel Meacham died in 1847, at the comparatively young age of fifty-two. But it may be truthfully said that he lived half a century ahead of his time, and accomplished more than the average man would have in three times his span of years. In the fame and recognition which the Big Cheese won for him and the Town of Sandy Creek, he created for himself a monument far more enduring than any of graven marble or granite could ever be.

A PROFESSOR OF WOODSOLOGY

Extending along the west and south flanks of Tug Hill, Redfield Township could always boast of possessing some of the most rugged country to be found anywhere west of the Adirondacks. In the old days its streams and woods abounded in speckled trout, game of various kinds, and furbearers galore, so quite naturally it had its full complement of famous hunters and trappers. Ranking high on this list was an individual known the country over as Billy Ward, but who came into the world sometime during the early '80s as William Ward Caster.

Born at a time when education was considered in the backwoods as something that could either be taken or left alone, Billy decided on the latter course and went through life barely able to read or write his own name. But in the things that were considered of paramount importance to his way of life, he was a veritable professor. No one knew better how to lure a wary old trout from its lair deep in the alders or from under that big, flat rock; no eye was keener in following the evasive trail of fox, buck, or bear; no one possessed greater skill in placing a Newhouse trap or rigging a deadfall in just the right spot to end the wanderings of mink, coon, or beaver. With a shotgun he was very proficient, but with a rifle he was deadly.

9

Preferring his carefree existence to a life of matrimonial bliss, Bill never married, but went through his entire life as an "old batch." Mainly, he made his living by hunting, fishing, and trapping. In the fall seasons, when the city sports ventured forth into the hills of Redfield and Osceola, he often served as a guide. Sometimes he took jobs in logging camps or sawmills, but only at such times as would not interfere with his main vocations. Some hinted that Bill occasionally carried on an illicit traffic in venison and brook trout, but this was only hearsay as far as the conservation authorities were concerned, and was never proved.

If this latter fact were so, it was not because the conservation authorities did not try. Time after time they sent special agents, posing as sports, summer campers, or timber cruisers, into the territory in an effort to pin some infraction of the game laws upon Billy or some of the other natives. With these gentry, Billy crossed swords in a never-ending battle of wits which developed many amusing sidelights.

One time he was deer hunting away down toward the High Falls of Mad River when he ran across a couple of these special game wardens. Now even if news of these strangers had not already been broadcast on the local grapevine, he would have recognized them for what they were. Most of the oldtimers could scent a government man like a fox could smell out a deer-mouse, and Billy's sense of smell was as keen as any in this respect.

As it was, he knew that these two fellows had been holed up in an old lumber camp a mile or so away; presumably hunting but actually doing a lot of snooping around. Putting on a disarmingly simple front, Billy stopped to chat with them.

"You fellers had any luck yet?" he inquired.

10

The strangers replied that they had not. "Haven't even had any camp meat yet," one of them informed him disgustedly. "Begins to look like we'll have to go home empty-handed. We've sure been hoping to take back a couple of nice bucks."

Billy let this remark pass and continued to discuss such safe subjects as the weather and general game conditions. One of the men offered Bill a drink from his pocket-flask, which was readily accepted; and by the end of a few minutes time he and the two men had become quite chummy.

As he was turning to leave, one of the fellows remarked casually, "Don't know of anyone who might fix us up with something to take home, do you?"

Billy considered this for a moment.

"Tell you what," he said finally. "You fellers been nice to me. Come up an' see me 'fore you go home. Live up towards Union Church. Ever'body knows me. Just ask for Billy Ward Caster."

At the mention of this name the game wardens mentally pricked up their ears. This was one of the men that they had been especially warned to be on the lookout for.

"Wait," said one. "We might be leaving tomorrow. Got anything hanging up now?"

Billy shook his head. "Nope, not right now," he said with a sly wink. "Just got rid of a couple nice ones, though. Might take me a couple days to stock up ag'in. Only thing I got now is a nice dry doe I shot coupla hours ago. Figger to pick her up on my way home. Well, so long. See you in a couple days."

Well, you probably have guessed what happened next. Just as Billy had planned, those two special wardens didn't intend to let him out of their sight, and he made it absurdly easy for them to accomplish their purpose. He must have been bubbling over with mirth as he strode along at an easy gait, never looking back or giving any sign that he knew he was being followed.

But had they been better acquainted with the territory, they would have noticed that Bill was taking an awfully long way home, just as they would have known that it wasn't necessary for him to plow through quite all of those tag-alder swamps and windfalls.

However, they kept on following, momentarily expecting to catch their man in red-handed possession of that illegal doe. After a couple of hours of this they began to suspect that they had been duped, but by this time they had no idea of where they were, and their only hope of getting out was to keep Billy in sight.

As for Billy, he still strode along seemingly unaware that there was another soul in the whole wide woods. At last, when it was almost dark, he suddenly disappeared from the sight of his pursuers. While they were discussing just what to do next, he suddenly stepped out of a clump of brush a few paces from them.

"Well, well," said Bill. "You fellers is quite a stretch from camp, ain't you?"

One of the men started on a lame explanation of how they had gotten lost and wandered a good deal. Bill waved this aside.

"Sure lucky I found you," he said. "Only a few minutes walk out to my place. From there you can follow the road back to your camp. Good walkin' an' only about twelve mile. Orta make it by ten, 'leven o'clock."

There was only one thing that the sadly disillusioned wardens could do, and they did it. They followed Billy out to his place and took the road home.

"And say boys," Billy drawled as they began the long,

weary hike, "when you git back to Albany, give the gov'nor my best regards."

Like many another of his day, Billy had an inordinate taste for strong drink; and when in his cups he dearly loved to sit with a bunch of drinking companions and regale them hour after hour with tales of his adventures. Many of these stories were known to be based on facts, but some others were suspected to be figments of an active imagination, conjured up for entertainment purposes only.

Be that as it may, it was said to have been as much fun as a three-ring circus when Bill launched into one of his story-telling sprees. His picturesque speech was always comical enough, but when abetted by the pantomime and mimicry of a natural-born comic, the effect became riotous. The writer has had many of these tales related to him by acquaintances of Billy's, but in passing them on, has no hope of re-creating their original amusing highlights.

"Boys," said Bill, hunching forward in his chair and measuring with his eye the depth of the red-eye in the glass before him, "Don't let no one tell you that bears is hard to walk up on. 'Member once I walked right up an' shook hands with one, an' perty near got shot for doin' it."

The place was Falvey's Hotel in Redfield, and the occasion was one Saturday night when Bill had come to town to lay in his weekly rations, both solid and liquid. The bar-room was crowded with local citizens, lumberjacks, and weekenders who had come to try their luck on the many trout streams in the vicinity. Sensing one of Billy's famous anecdotes, the crowd gathered around, and several more drinks appeared like magic on the table before him.

13

"I'd been fishin' the River (Mad) down towards Otter Mills," resumed Billy. "Had perty good luck, too, but finely the danged flies an' skeeters (here a flurry of hands and arms as though driving off swarms of the pests) got so ornery that I had to give up with only thirty-forty trout in my basket. Well, sir, I took off crosslots through the woods, tryin' to outrun the devils.

"Perty soon I come out in the old Cherry Hill Clearin', couple mile back of my house. Place was all growed up to weeds and brush, with lots of choke-cherry bushes around the old cellar holes where the houses had been tore down.

"Well sir, just as I was about to go bustin' out into that clearin' a thrashin' in them choke-cherry bushes caught my eye, an' I 'cided to 'vestigate. I sneaked around a little, an' perty soon I could see an old boar bear bendin' the bushes down an' scoopin' the cherries into his mouth with both hands. (Here a pantomime of the beast's motions that brought a roar of merriment from the crowd.)

"The cherries was ripe an' must've tasted perty good, 'cause that old feller was so busy he didn't pay no 'tention to me at all. Well sir, I watched him for maybe four-five minutes, an' was just about to go on about my own dang business when a idea struck me right 'twixt the eyes. S'I to myself, 'Billy Boy, how close you s'pose you kin git to that old boy without him seein' you?'

"Well, I snuck around to t'other side of the clearin' so's to git downwind, as I knowed he'd be sure to smell that oil-tar an' citronelly I had on for fly-dope. Then I started crawlin' up on him. (Here Billy got down on all fours and began a cautious stalk, carefully circling chairs and tables instead of trees and bushes.) You know, that old feller was havin' himself such a good time that I

14

sneaked right up to him. There he stood on his hind feet, with his back towards me an' not more'n six foot away.

"Don't know whatever possessed me to do it. Mighta got my face slapped good'n' hard. Anyway, I stepped right up, give him a helluva slap right 'twixt the shoulders, an' hollered, "What the Hell you doin' here?""

Billy paused to take a long drink from one of the glasses, then closed his eyes and settled back in his chair. After a while someone got curious and asked, "What happened then, Bill?"

"Well sir," resumed Billy, "right then I certain got the surprise of my life. Quick as lightnin' that old boy spun around, an' went 'Whoof.' Had his mouth chuck full of choke-cherry stones, an' he let me have the hull charge right smack in the face. Like buckshot, they was, an' they knocked me flatter'n a cow-flop. Didn't come to until nigh onto dark. To make things all the worse, the old devil opened up my fish-baskit an' et up all my trout afore he left. Teached me to mind my own damn business, I can tell you. Boys, don't ever monkey aroun' with an old boar bear in choke-cherry season."

Another story that Billy loved to tell also concerned an adventure with a bear. This one was obviously a tale designed for amusement only. Billy didn't expect anyone to believe it, and nobody did; but that never prevented him from telling it whenever a good opportunity presented itself.

"Happened once when I was huntin' up in the Adirondack Mountings," reminisced Billy. "Was sneakin' careful-like along a little narrow trail, with a mounting on one side an' a danged gully two-three hundred foot deep on t'other. Well sir, I stepped around a bend in that there trail, an' come face to face with the biggest, an' blackest, an' ugliest lookin' bear I ever seen in all my

15

borned days. Looked to be a good axe-handle length 'twixt the eyes, an' about 'leven foot tall. He didn't act none like he intended to step aside an' let me have the trail, an' I didn't see no way I could give it up to him.

"Back in them days I was fast as a chipmunk, an' quicker'n a wink I up with that old 45/90 Winchester I was carryin'. Just as he let out a yowl an' started over to shake hands with me, I let him have it smack in the middle of his chest. An' boys, I never come so close to gettin' shot in all my life as I did right then.

"Hadn't no more'n cut loose when 'Peeengg,' a bullet hits the rock alongside of my head. Kinda discombooberated me for a second, an' I scootched down thinkin' someone had took a shot at me. But nothin' else happened, an' by the time I got straightened around ag'in the bear was gone outta sight.

"Well, I slid in another ca'tridge an' started lookin' around. Found blood, an' perty soon I found the bear, deader'n hell. Had a hole plumb through him, front to back.

"Took me a few minutes to figger out where that bullet had come from, though. But after a while it come to me. 'T wa'nt no *other* bullet at all, but the one I'd fired myself that perty near lifted my top-knot. You see, a 45/90 bullet travels kinda slow, an' that danged bear turned clean around while it was goin' through him. When it come out his back 'twas p'inted right smack at me, an' I'm mighty lucky to be here today, waitin' for you fellers to buy the drinks."

16

SMARTVILLE

Smartville is a name which at one time denoted a lively and thriving community, but today indicates only a four-corners on the map. Situated very nearly in the center of Boylston Township, where the Lacona-State Road and the Orwell-Boylston Center roads cross, it once was a veritable bee-hive of enterprise and industry. At present, only six houses and the town highway barn remain there.

The first settler in the place was Israel Putnam Smart, who came there as a young man from Scriba, N. Y., bringing his wife and family with him. This was during the 1850s and the territory was then very wild. A lumberman by trade, Mr. Smart was attracted by the magnificent stands of virgin timber in the area, and purchased a large tract of land northeast of where the village came into existence.

After a few years he built and operated a large sawmill where Trout Brook crossed the highway. This was originally water-powered, but was later converted to steam; still later, he built a barrel-stave and hoop mill, which was operated in conjunction with the sawmill for many years.

As they grew into manhood, Mr. Smart's two sons, both of whom possessed unusual mechanical abilities, joined him in the business. The older of these sons, William, was later the inventor of the famous Smart Steam Wagon, an account of which is included elsewhere

17

in this book. The younger son, Fred, moved to Lacona after the decline of the family interests in Smartville at which place he operated a prosperous wagon and boat shop for many years, also manufacturing sleighs and cutters as a sideline.

The original Smart sawmill was connected with the timberlands by a tram-road some two miles in length. This was made by fastening long, slender poles several inches in diameter, to bed-pieces set into the ground; the poles serving as rails on which ran the deeply-grooved wheels of the tram cars or wagons. This method rendered it much faster and easier to transfer the logs from the woods to the millyard.

As the Smart enterprises grew and employed more and more men, it became necessary to provide living quarters for some of the employees. At first, several small and temporary houses were built, but later Mr. Smart constructed a large utility building known for many years as the Arcade. This stood about halfway up the hill just east of the four-corners, on the north or left side of the road leading toward Redfield. Old sources picture it as a long, rambling, frame building; sided and roofed with hand-shaved shingles. The west end was devoted to a boarding house in which many of the company's men were quartered, also a company store which was kept stocked with most of the staple commodities of the times. The rest of the building was divided into several apartments for the use of employees with families.

Later, other industries began to develop and soon quite a sizeable little settlement had materialized. Albert Dykes established a blacksmith shop, and soon after a cheese-factory was built, being supplied with milk by farmers who moved in and cleared lands for agriculture.

18

A butter-tub shop and a plate factory were put into operation.

By this time the need for a school was acutely felt, so one was built and a young lady by the name of Polly Alport was installed as teacher. This was the only school for miles around, and in lieu of a church it was also used as a meeting-house on Sundays.

A very amusing tale is told concerning an incident that occurred during one of these religious services. Actual names cannot be used in its telling, because many descendants of the family involved still live throughout the general area.

It seems that a group of Baptists were using the school building as a meeting-house, the preacher being a young man of very Irish descent who worked in a sawmill during the week. Now this young preacher had not always been a Baptist. In his childhood home, just across the St. Lawrence River in Canada, he had been reared in the old Irish tradition as a Roman Catholic, as had all the rest of his family since time immemorial. But something had happened to cause him to "turn his coat," as the old saying went, and he had embraced the Protestant faith and become a minister of the Gospel.

Of course this had caused great bitterness and he had broken off all family ties, migrating south and leaving behind his parents and many brothers and sisters. Settling at Smartville, he did very well for himself, and soon was conducting the Sunday services for a group of followers of his faith, whom he organized into the semblance of a church group.

In the meantime one of his brothers, joining the general influx of Canadian emigres into New York State, had also entered the area; and unbeknown to the minister, had bought a farm a few miles away. Then he re-

19

turned to Canada to bring back a herd of cattle that he owned there.

These cattle were not brought across until after cold weather had set in, when they were driven over the ice and along the northern roads toward their destination.

Now it just happened that this procession reached the village of Smartville on a Sunday forenoon, at the very time when the Baptists were right smack in the middle of their services. It being a rather mild day, the meeting-house door had been left slightly ajar to somewhat mitigate the heat generated by the big, wood-burning stove.

Just as the herd of cattle and their drovers reached the heart of the village and a point opposite the meeting-house, a half-grown calf which had been following its mother became frightened by a dog, and leaving the herd, dashed madly through the half-open door, scattering worshippers right and left in its wild flight.

Close behind the calf came its highly irritated owner, probably also scattering a few choice words that seemed utterly out of place in a sedate church meeting; to come suddenly face to face with a despised brother whom he had not known until that moment to be anywhere within miles.

For a moment an icy silence gripped the room, as the two surprised but unrelenting brothers each mentally evaluated the situation. Then, the calf having been subdued by several pairs of ready hands, its owner grasped it by the neck and pushed it toward the door.

"Come on, you poor, damned, misguided beast," he said in a cold and bitter voice. "Don't tell me you've gone and turned your coat too."

During the next few years Smartville attracted a diversity of enterprises, among them being even a pill factory. This stood east of the corners almost across from the Arcade, and was conducted by a man named Henry Schermerhorn (or Scammyhorn), it being a one-man operation most of the time. Old-timers used to tell amusing tales of how "Doc" Scammyhorn concocted his pills from various herb extracts combined with a flour dough. The pellets were formed by swiftly rolling little gobs of the mixture between his hands, after which they were dried and coated with sugar.

One of the properties of these pellets was supposed to be a very potent cathartic action, but the tale is told that one day a pet rooster owned by a neighbor came upon a batch of newly-rolled pellets drying in the sun, and gobbled down the whole lot without any apparent after effects, either for the better or the worse.

Here also was manufactured a salve that was known far and wide for its unparalleled healing qualities. Composed of ingredients known only to its maker, it was put up in semi-solid sticks about three inches long and an inch in diameter, protected by a heavily oiled paper wrapper. When an end of the stick was held over the flame of a match or candle it quickly softened to a consistency which could easily be applied to a bandage and placed on an injury. No matter what the injury was . . . cuts, bruises, strains, or burns . . . "Scammyhorn's Salve" could, (and in all fairness, usually did) cure them all.

For many years this product and "Scammyhorn's Pills" were household names throughout the northern counties of the state. They were dispensed to the public by a younger brother of their maker, Abe Schermerhorn, who usually traveled by horse and wagon.

This Abe was something of a character in his own right, and known to be quite wealthy for the times. It was said that he made considerable money by conducting

21

a fairly active mortgage brokerage, buying and selling indebtedness whenever and wherever a dollar could be made. He also loaned money, at usurious but in those days perfectly legal, interest rates. Today he would probably be prosecuted as a loan shark; but in those days of catch-as-catch-can financial standards he waxed prosperous, if unloved by some of his clients.

For many years the road east out of Smartville did not connect with the road between Lorraine and Redfield, commonly known as the Old State — or Military Road. About a mile of dense forest intervened between the two, and during the early '70's the town let a contract to a man named Charley Beech to cut a right-of-way through for the building of a connecting link.

Being a very industrious and ambitious worker, Mr. Beech set out to do the whole job by himself, falling the trees and clearing the brush by the use of nothing but an axe. In order that he might spend all the time possible on the job, Mrs. Beech used to carry a lunch to him at noon. One day she arrived a little early, and Beech, not noticing her approach, felled a large tree on her and she was instantly killed.

In spite of this and other bad luck, he went ahead to finish the task, and the road was built to connect with the State Road where St. Joseph's Catholic Church was later constructed. The stretch of forest through which he labored is still known as the Beech Woods, and the hill near which Mrs. Beech met her death is called "The Charley Choppin' Hill."

For many years it was whispered darkly among the older and more superstitious element of the surrounding populace, that sometimes at night on the anniversaries of the death of Mrs. Beech, a patient listener might hear the crash of a falling tree, accompanied by the shrieks of fear and anguish as it crushed the luckless woman to the ground.

However true the accounts of these ghastly sounds might have been the author cannot say, as they were supposed to have happened many years before his time, and no similar happenings have been reported in a long time. But it is a well known fact that trees sometimes fall all by themselves and for no apparent reason; and screech-owls often rend the night's stillness with cries that well might be mistaken for the wail of a banshee or departed spirit.

By 1893 the population of the village and surrounding territory had grown to a size where a post-office was deemed advisable, and one was established there during that year, with Theophilius Lenoir installed as the first post-master. However, this office never attained any great size or importance, and a few years later was abandoned as unsatisfactory.

During the first few years of the Smart enterprise, the lumber, timbers, and other products of the mills were transported to Lacona for shipment to various markets on the old Rome, Watertown, and Ogdensburgh Railroad. At first the transportation was accomplished by the use of teams and wagons, but this method was slow and costly, and not in keeping with the progressive ideas of the younger generation of Smarts.

Accordingly, young Will put on his thinking cap and came up with the idea for the steam wagon; an innovation that soon proved its worth and became a distinct boon in the advancement of the family fortunes.

During the years succeeding the turn of the century, Smartville went into a slump from which it never recovered. One by one the mills and factories closed down and disappeared. The old Arcade burned, as did some of the other buildings. The last industry to succumb was a cheese factory located just past the four corners on the road to Boylston Center, which was last operated by a Mrs. Clemons, one of the very few lady cheese-makers in the history of the state.

Only one of the fine houses built by the Smart family during the height of their influence still remains. This is the one built by Fred, the younger son, for his own personal dwelling house after he married, and was at one time a beautifully finished and pleasantly located residence. This house was for many years owned and occupied by Mr. and Mrs. Fred Delong. Mr. Delong operated a large and productive farm there for many years, and was a long-time supervisor of the town; but after his death the place gradually fell into disrepair and is now unoccupied.

Today, Smartville's one-time glory is all but forgotten, and it is now merely a cross-roads in a community of farms that, like the village they supplanted, are slowly sinking into oblivion.

THE SMART
STEAM WAGON

Probably the most ingenious contraption ever to enter the hills of Boylston, in northern Oswego County, was the famous Smart Steam Wagon. Certainly it was the most picturesque and awe-inspiring as it traveled the road from Smartville to Lacona, hauling five or six large wagon-loads of lumber behind, spewing smoke, sparks, and cinders over the countryside.

This ponderous vehicle first had its conception in the inventive brain of William Smart, who with his father Israel and his brother Fred, owned and operated a large lumbering operation, sawmill, and stave-mill at Smartville, about five miles east of Lacona. Economic necessity, rather than hope of any monetary gain from patent rights, seems to have been the incentive for the original idea; as there is no record of Mr. Smart ever having patented the invention.

In those days of the 1870's the roads in Boylston, as in veritably every other rural community in the north country, were rocky and rough; and in spring and fall, beset with seas of mud. In addition, the Smartville-Lacona route embraced the Wheat Hill, which was in itself quite an elevation, and the First and Second Gulfs, whose steep-sided depths had never been bridged. The road just dropped in one side and climbed out the other.

These facts made the hauling of lumber from the

Smart mills to the railroad at Lacona a slow, laborious, and expensive operation. A team of horses or oxen pulling a loaded wagon could make about one round trip a day; what with "chaining" on the downgrades and "blocking" on the upgrades. This necessitated the hiring of many teams and drivers to transport the output of the mills, thus cutting sharply into the profits from the business.

To the progressive-minded Mr. Smart it seemed that there should be some way to alter this situation, and straightaway he set about to find it. After a great deal of thought and discussion on the matter, there gradually evolved in his fertile mind plans for a steam-powered vehicle which, he believed, would revolutionize the transportation problem.

At first the elder Smart, who was the actual founder and real boss of the family enterprise, took a dim view of the project. Being of a more conservative makeup than his son, he could not see how it could possibly be a success. Horse-power had served him in his business for many years; horse-power would have to suffice in this instance, expensive though it might be. As a consequence he flatly refused both his consent and financial aid in the development of what he considered to be a hare-brained scheme.

However, this did not mar the determination of the younger man to go ahead with his plans. As he went about his daily duties the idea was always at the back of his mind, and night after night he spent long hours working out one detail after another. At once it became apparent to his practical mind that a long and cumbersome horizontal boiler would not be suitable. One of the newer and more compact upright types would have to be used, and it would have to be adapted to burning

26

wood, of which his family had a cheap and almost limit-less supply.

After the detail work came more long nights of work on drawings and specifications.

At last the elder Smart, seeing that his son would not be thwarted in the realization of his dream, gave his consent and promise of financial backing, and commissioned the young man to go ahead with the enterprise. Armed with a completed set of working drawings and an unquenchable desire to see the project through, young Will set out to find a builder.

"I don't know how long I'll be gone," he confided to Levi Crandall, keeper of the old Arcade boarding house in Smartville, "But when I come back I'll bring a machine that will really make folks sit up and take notice, and put Smartville on the map."

The Ames Iron Works at Oswego, makers of steam engines and boilers, was selected to carry out the actual building of the wagon. After considerable consultation between Will and the Ames engineers, it was decided that the plans he had evolved were workable and could be used with very little revision, and work on the project began.

This consumed nearly all of one winter, and finally, in the early spring of 1879, the steam wagon was pronounced ready for its initial tests. These were conducted in the city of Oswego, and needless to say, excited a great deal of interest and wonder. A newspaper article in the Oswego *Paladium-Times* of that date tells of the incident, describing the speed of the vehicle as ". . . about that of an Oswego horse-car on a Sunday when there is a ball-game on." This must have meant about six miles an hour, as that was the average speed of its travel. Apparently it made very little difference whether or not a load was being hauled, as the machine had been designed for utility and power rather than speed.

In appearance, the vehicle was about the size and shape of a railroad flat-car, and was also about as ponderous and heavy. It had three massive wheels, the two in back being heavily cleated with iron to assist it in clawing up the steep and rocky grades. The third wheel, set in the middle of the front end, was connected to a steering apparatus which was activated by a huge- iron steering-wheel. This was built with hand-holds projecting from it to aid in the application of the real muscle-power needed to turn it.

On the front half of the platform was located the steam boiler and engine, protected at least partially from the weather by an iron canopy top, and just back of this was storage room for the fuel supply. There were no facilities for shifting gears; the power being transmitted direct from engine to gears to rear axle and wheels. The back half of the apparatus was used as cargo space, and when loaded this added weight contributed greatly to the traction of the wheels.

With the tests completed and the machine declared ready for operation, the young inventor now had to consider the problem of getting it to Smartville, over thirty long miles away. Undaunted, he hired a crew of helpers and set out. It is said to have been a wonderful sight to see as they went puffing and chugging along the country roads, belching great clouds of smoke and steam that scared horses and cattle, and in some cases the settlers themselves, half out of their wits.

Early in the planning stages, Mr. Smart had realized that most of the bridges along the route would have to be reinforced, and some even rebuilt. With this in mind he hauled behind him several wagons loaded with

28

heavy hardwood planks and other building material. On coming to a bridge the cavalcade would pause while planks were laid over the structure and props were placed under its beams, after which a slow and cautious crossing was effected. If everything went well, the planks were reloaded and the entourage proceeded merrily on its way to the next bridge.

Even with these precautions, several of the smaller and weaker bridges failed to stand the weight, and these of course had to be rebuilt before going on. All this took up a great deal of time, and it was not until evening of the third day that the apparatus finally began the last lap of its journey, the five bridgeless miles between Lacona and Smartville.

These last miles were traveled under a full head of steam, the smokestack shooting sparks into the gathering darkness of the mild spring evening, and the whistle setting echoes racing through the rugged Boylston hills in a wild paean of victory for a returning son. People rushed from their homes to gaze in rapt wonder as the fearful contraption thundered past.

Warned by the blasting whistle, nearly everyone able to run, walk, or crawl was on hand when the outfit pulled into Smartville. Levi Crandall years later told that it was a wonderful sight, for that day and age, as it steamed majestically into the mill-yard, pulling its wagons loaded with wildly shouting people. The celebration put on by the excited inhabitants ran far into the night, and must have seemed very satisfying indeed to the young man responsible for it.

With the initial enthusiasm over, the steam wagon speedily began to vindicate the soundness of its inventor's ideas by the vastly increased hauling capacity which it made possible. Instead of one, it could make four or five round trips to the railroad in a day, hauling five and sometimes six wagon loads of lumber each time. Soon the use of teams in hauling the company's products was dispensed with entirely. For several years the machine continued to operate from spring until late fall, playing an important role in the rise of the Smart family to the affluence which they came to enjoy.

What eventually became of the invention is not definitely known. Some believe that Mr. Smart took it with him when he later went to Tennessee to carry on lumbering operations there. Be that as it may, its fame has filtered down through the years to make the name of Will Smart something to be remembered.

TUG HILL SENDS HER
SONS TO WAR

Today we know it as the Civil War, but at the time of its being it was referred to as "The War of the Rebellion," or more simply as "The Rebellion." However it was known, it is an indisputable fact that this holocaust of destruction that swept the nation like a breath of purifying flame, pitting former friend against friend and brother against brother, leaving hardly a family intact and untouched, had an unprecedented impact on the lives of virtually every community east of the Mississippi River.

Like all the rest, the towns and villages of the Tug Hill watershed felt their share of this impact, and responded in the traditional American pattern.

Few indeed of the men and boys who went forth to do their bit understood the underlying causes of the conflict, or the political aspects involved therein. Few cared. What they did know was that their country was threatened and had asked for their help, and they were quick to answer. Their faith was in God and the Union, and this faith sustained them and carried them through to ultimate victory.

It would be virtually impossible, and if possible would require a tome of gigantic proportions, to record all of the deeds of daring and heroism, the moments of triumph and defeat, of joy and pathos, experienced by

31

these young farmers and lumberjacks, these bear hunters and river-drivers, these sawmill hands and trappers and bark-peelers, who made up the rank and file of the regiments from the Tug Hill Country.

However, it is still possible to trace some of the activities of a representative few who lived in the Boylston-Orwell-Sandy Creek area, by letters, diaries, and journals that they left behind. And it is safe to assume that, taken by and large, their experiences represented a fair cross-section of the everyday lives of these honored vetrans from the entire region. Today, when not one participant of the great conflict remains alive to tell their story, these records should be preserved and cherished as national treasures.

From a journal kept by the mother of a young soldier (who happily returned to her unharmed) comes the following description of the stirring times at the beginning of the war:

Excitement ran high in Sandy Creek in the spring of 1861, following President Lincoln's call for volunteers, and as was the case throughout the country, the young men were prompt to answer. War meetings were held in churches and schoolhouses, and the leading orators of the day gave their services freely in promoting the formation of companies.

In each town was a war committee of two men, who drove through the countryside, stopping at various farms where there were young men, and urging them to enlist. They would give notice of a meeting to be held at some central point in the near future, and urge all to be present.

All over the country the scenes were the same. The women, looking out of the houses, would see a committee member in conversation with their men-folks, and when the latter came in from work, the feminine members of the household would ask the purpose of the visit, although they already knew and dreaded the answer. "I wish you wouldn't enlist," they would say. When the men had enlisted and were leaving for Oswego or Syracuse or some similar point to be mustered into the service, came the saddest scenes of all. The women wept as they said goodbye to husband, sweetheart, brother, or son, and many said, "We will never see them again."

John J. Hollis, a member of Co. C, 110th Regiment, used to relate the circumstances under which he enlisted. He was living at his father's home in the town of Orwell, and was working in the field with a friend, (Willis S. Samson, grandfather of the author) when Mr. Parker, a member of the war committee, came by. Stopping his horse, he asked the boys if they had ever thought of enlisting. They admitted that they had, and he informed them that there was to be a war meeting that night in the Hemlock Schoolhouse in Boylston, and invited them to be present.

In company with many others from Orwell, they attended the meeting. Mr. Parker informed them what the quota for Orwel had been set at, and told them that they would be credited to their own town, even though they enlisted in Boylston. When they left for home that night they had enlisted to serve for a period of three years. (Note: The records of the 110th Infantry Regiment as published in the Oswego County history, list the enlistment date of John J. Hollis as Aug. 4, 1862, and that of Willis S. and Levi C. Samson as Aug. 6, 1862, in spite of the fact that Mr. Hollis often asserted that they enlisted together. All were members of Co. C).

The Sunday before they left for Oswego to be mustered into service, the minister at the Orwell church announced that he would hold a special service for the boys who had enlisted. They sat together in the front of the church, and the reverend spoke very eloquently and tenderly to them.

The neighbors turned out to take the boys to Oswego, the trip being made in democrat wagons and buckboards. The young men would ride for a few miles over the rough roads, and then get out and walk a while to rest their aching bones and muscles.

Levi Crandall, who lived just south of Sandy Creek, was a boy of ten at the start of the war, and loved to relate happenings of the times, and how they made an impression on his mind that he could never forget. He had older brothers and sisters, and when the call came for volunteers, there was a Crandall boy ready and eager to go.

"I shall never forget the morning that my brother went away to war," Mr. Crandall would relate. "He seemed so young, and yet a hero in my eyes. He said to father that he was ready to go, and father would not stop him. My father was a wonderful man with his children. I knew it was breaking his heart to see his boy go, but not a word was spoken.

"It came time for my brother to go to Oswego to join the others in the service, and he would have gone in with the others, but father said, 'No, I want to take you and will drive in with our own team.' It was a long trip from our farm to Oswego and back with a team of horses, so father was up early the next morning. The chores were done and father got the team ready and harnessed. We all helped to hitch them to the democrat buggy, each one wanting to help.

"When the team was hitched up, father drove up to the kitchen door, where we always got into the rigs, and

34

in a cheery voice called out to inquire if the boy was ready. The boy was, and I can see father now as he raised his hand and motioned for us to be quiet. He knelt down on the bare kitchen floor, there by the door, and began praying for that boy who was to go. I can still hear his voice today as it comes back over a span of seventy years, and I can repeat some of his words asking that the boy be shielded from harm and if possible brought home again. With the prayer over there were quick goodbyes, and the team drove off on the long trip to Oswego.

"That boy did come home again after a full term in the service. But that scene in the farm kitchen on the morning that he left I shall never forget."

The 24th New York Volunteers was the first Oswego County regiment mustered into service, and Co. G was composed almost entirely of men from Sandy Creek, Boylston, Orwell, and Richland. Its officers were as follows: Captain, William T. Ferguson, Sandy Creek; First Lieutenant, Calvin Burch, Orwell; Second Lieutenant, Henry B. Corse, Sandy Creek. Members killed in action were: Henry Corse, William Hollis, Mason Parish, Duane Damon, Mattison Samson (Second Bull Run), Mervin Olmstead, Ezra Balch, Almarian Clark, and Philo Bass. Wounded: Vincent DeLong, Clay Cass, Gardiner Hollis, Wm. Reemer, Allen Boss, John Lattimer, and Lieutenant Calvin Burch.

David Hamer, who prior to the war lived in Boylston, and was a member of Co. G, 24th Infantry, wrote in his memoirs:

"It would seem but right to say a word here in regard to the boys who composed the two Companies G and K, from Sandy Creek and Belleville. They were farmer boys and all very green and awkward in drill and military movement, on the formation of the 24th Regiment; while those from Oswego had mostly been members of the old Oswego Guards and were very proficient in drill previous to enlisting. The result was that the two companies were dubbed 'Greenhorns' and 'Cowboys,' while those from Boylston were called 'Ox-drivers' and 'Gum-chewers,' (note: the latter term derived from the habit of chewing spruce gum). In consequence, some very hard feelings resulted at first."

'But things changed; all learned the drill and the experience of the campaign proved that these boys were equal, if not superior to, their city cousins. Even the gum-chewers performed very well at the front. They were at home in the woods and swamps as well as in the cleared fields. All had been familiar with guns before leaving home, and were now admitted to be among the bravest and the best, as well as producing some of the best sharpshooters in the entire army.

"The terrible losses that they sustained attested to the recklessness with which they fought, and the feeling in the regiment was that those who remained should be taken into close communion."

Among an impressive number of notable engagements, the 24th New York Volunteers fought at the Battle of Antietam Creek, and Mr. Hamer's memoirs gave a first-hand account of the bloody conflict, he having been a participant.

"Company G of Sandy Creek had but seven, or at most eight, men in the fight. The first man to fall in old Co. G was Martin J. Dennison of Orwell. He was struck by a bullet across the forehead, fracturing the skull and bringing him to the ground. He soon began to show signs of life, and was assisted to his feet by A. R. Penfield (later a lumber dealer in Oswego City), as brave a

36

man as ever drew rifle to his eye, and one who always had a kind word for a fellow soldier. He told Dennison to keep his hand to his forehead to keep the blood from running into his eyes, and to go to the rear as soon as possible.

"Next in turn came Moreau J. Salisbury of Sandy Creek, struck by a bullet in the ankle or instep, which passed out through the heel, making a fearful wound. He was helped to the rear by David Crocker. The next struck was Merrick Salisbury, also of Sandy Creek, a son of Lorenze Salisbury. He was struck by a musket ball which lodged in the knee joint under the knee pan, inflicting a very painful wound. Thomas Cox, now an engineer on the Rome and Watertown Railroad, is, I think, the one who helped to carry him back out of the way and from under the fire.

"Next in turn comes the lamented Lyman Haughton, of Orwell, of whom too much cannot be said in his favor. He was twenty-three years of age and had the strength and courage of a tiger, a splendid form six feet high, iron nerves, and was Number I in the use of the Enfield rifle. Capt. Dan O'Brien told me just before he died that it was Haughton who shot and killed the rebel general, Stark."

Mason and Lorenze Salisbury, the fathers of the two wounded Salisbury boys already mentioned, were in Washington during the Battle of Antietam, and were able to see the wounded carried back. Both found their sons among the desperately wounded. Who can describe the meeting; the joy at finding them alive and the sorrow that they were wounded?

"When the time came for their wounds to be dressed, the surgeons decided that amputation was necessary to save their lives. The knives are ready and the surgeons

37

are waiting, but Mason is pleading to save his boy's limb, and thinks that with the proper care it may be saved. The surgeon tells him that there is not one chance in ten of saving the boy's life. Still the father pleads to save him. At last the surgeon tells him to take the boy away from there and do the best he can for him.

"Next comes Merrick Salisbury, a brave boy with a musket ball lodged in the knee joint. It cannot be extracted as it is imbedded in the bone. The surgeon tells the father that it is a clear case that the leg must come off. Lorenze objects to it, and cites the case of Mason as a precedent. He is finally allowed to take the boy, but on going the doctor tells him that the boy cannot live to exceed five days in that condition. If I remember right, within that time Lorenze started for home with him, a corpse.

"Moreau Salisbury, who had the best of care that could be given him under the circumstances, lingered between life and death for months. But with a strong hold on life, and a constitution of iron, he finally pulled through."

Another example of a father's devotion to a wounded son was touchingly displayed by a man named Ira West, who during the Civil War lived just south of Sandy Creek village.

Mr. West enlisted early in the war, and served out his regular period of time, after which he was returned home because of ill health. Soon after this his son, Milo, a boy of eighteen, also enlisted. The first word that the parents had of their son's enlistment was received in a letter from Rome, N. Y., in which he stated that he had married and enlisted from that place.

Upon hearing of this, the father immediately reenlisted, hoping that he could be placed in the same regi-

38

ment, and that he might be able to look after his son. This hope did not materialize. He was placed in another regiment, but in this regiment was also placed young Albert Howe, another eighteen-year old boy from Sandy Creek. Ira immediately appointed himself adviser and protector of young Albert, watching over him carefully. Perhaps this was sort of panacea for the disappointment of not being able to contact his own son.

Some time later the older man became ill, and was again parolled home, never having seen his son or received word of him. But while home on sick leave, he received a telegram stating that Milo was desperately wounded and just alive in a Washington hospital.

Ira West was a splendid walker, and this stood him in good stead when he immediately set out for Washington. Much railroad track had been torn up during the war, and when there was a long stretch where no trains could run, he walked.

By this method, Mr. West finally reached Washington, only to learn the bad news that his son had been buried in Arlington Cemetery only one hour before his arrival.

Weakened by sickness and the strain of the long journey, Mr. West was unable to go to Arlington, but went to the bed in the hospital where his son had died. Even in that short time, the bed had been taken by another wounded man. It was not until the end of the war and the return of the veterans that he was able to gain further word about the death of his son.

Among the many famous battles in which the Twenty-fourth New York Volunteers participated, the Battle of Manassas Junction, or Second Bull Run, stands out with startling clarity. It was here that many young men born and reared among the rugged hills and valleys of the Tug Hill plateau displayed their courage and audacity in deeds of heroism that should live forever. Here, too, many of them laid down their young lives in their country's defense, or left the field with painful wounds that would affect them for the remainder of their days.

The series of hit-and-run, advance-and-retreat engagements known as Second Bull Run, began on the twenty-eighth of August, 1862, and found the 24th supporting an artillery regiment in action near Manassas Junction. Orson Gale, a native of Orwell and a member of Co. G., told of his experience in this battle in these, his own words:

"At evening the regiment moved forward to harass the retreating foe. The red dust lay in suffocating thickness in the road through which we passed on the double-quick, stirring it up beneath our feet until it hung in great clouds about us, shrouding the landscape from view. Down the road we dashed, and through a creek, on the opposite bank of which, on his horse, sat General McDowell, hat in hand, with clenched fist menacing the air. As the regiment approached, he inquired:

"What regiment is that?"

"The Twenty-fourth New York," was the reply.

"Hurrah for the Twenty-fourth New York," the general shouted. "Give it to them, boys, give it to them! They are on the run, don't let them stop. Remember your country, and remember Bull Run!"

"An answering cheer rose from our lips, as through the suffocating dust we rushed along. Soon a retiring battery is met.

"What's the matter, boys?"

"Out of ammunition."

"Close up and forward. Forward, and away we go,

and still the twilight deepens and the shadows gather 'round.

"Suddenly an ominous flash of fire, and the report of artillery immediately in front, and the whiz and whistle of grape and canister greets our ears, and exploding shells burst among us.

"We immediately flank out of the road and into the bed of a creek, out of the immediate rake of their fire, until covered by the embankment of the creek, about ten feet in height, up which we scramble. No attempt at order then, and short time there was for organizing on its brow.

"The top of that bluff revealed a stone wall, from which hundreds of guns poured their murderous fire among us. Upon the rise of ground in front appeared a very wall of fire, and in the open brush and woods at the left was a large force of the enemy, and fire answering fire. Upward, forward, nothing fearing until the very crest of the hill is reached and bayonets crossed. Two brigades of intrepid, enthusiastic youths crossed bayonets with an army numbering sixty thousand men.

"Who could endure it? What amount of patriotism or love of country could stand in that holocaust of fire and death? Back, alas back. Slowly but surely back. Ah, what is that? Forth steps a youth, his pale face lighted up and made paler by the flashing lines of fire from three sides of that fatal square. His musket and his hat raised in front, his footsteps press forward, while back he casts his face and shouts, 'Be brave, men. Don't run like cowards. Forward, and follow me. I'll lead you.' 'Twas but a second, but many saw how Marvin Cozzens fell. (Note: Marvin Cozzens died Sept. 14, 1862, from wounds received here. On Oct. 5, 1862, Mattison Samson, Co. G, 24th Inf., also of Orwell, died of wounds received in the same engagement.)

"While like a wall came up the line of bristling bayonets, and the words from the hoarse throat of a mounted enemy officer rang out, 'Steady, steady Hampton Legion,' and on they passed over the dead and wounded and the dying. They passed, and backward we slowly yielded the ground, until darkness increased and threw its merciful folds over the scene of carnage, and silence reigned. So was the battle of Groveton fought and lost."

In this engagement the regiment lost twenty-nine killed, one hundred and eighty-six wounded, and one hundred and twenty-four missing. Among the killed was Major Andrew J. Barney of Ellisburg, former captain of Co. K, who died gallantly fighting at the head of his command.

Just as Oswego County had its 24th New York Volunteers, so did Jefferson County boast of her famous regiment raised almost entirely within her borders, and composed mostly of her native sons. This was the 35th Infantry, commonly known as "The Jefferson County Regiment," organized at Elmira on June 3, 1861. Co.'s A and E were recruited at Watertown, Co. C at Theresa, Co. G at Adams, Co. I at Redwood, and Co. K at Brownville. Several of these companies contained men who hailed from the rock-ribbed slopes of the Tug Hill plateau.

This organization served out its full three years, participating in many notable engagements, including Warrenton Springs, Gainesville, Second Bull Run, Chantilly, South Mountain, Antietam, and Fredrickburg, as well as several other small skirmishes.

It was disbanded at Elmira June 5, 1863. Of its original 1,250 members, only 593 were mustered out; 130 having been killed in battle, 70 deaths by disease, 90 discharged for wounds, 140 for disability, 227 missing in action.

Surely, no other tribute, beyond this record, is needed to testify to the daring, devotion to duty, and unswerving trust in God and country, displayed by the honored members of its distinguished rolls.

As prompt and satisfactory as had been the response to the original call for volunteers, when the first patriotic fervor had worn itself out, and reports of battle casualties began to filter back to the folks at home, it became apparent that the individual towns would be unable to fill their quotas by enlistments alone. Therefor, some sort of draft system would become necessary.

Accordingly, the War Department appointed in each Congressional district, a provost marshal, whose duty it was to administer the enrollment, determine the physical fitness, and decide on the acceptance or rejection for military duty, of all male residents between the ages of eighteen and forty-five. These officials in turn appointed sub-officials, consisting of an examining surgeon and assistant, deputy provost marshals, enrollment clerks, quartermasters, and several special agents, to help expedite their duties.

In this, as in every conflict in which the nation has ever been involved, there were many of draft age whose ideas of patriotism did not extend to leaving the safety of home and going to fight on a strange terrain, for a cause of which they understood very little. These men were perfectly content to let someone else do their share for them, and as news of the horrors of battle became more prevalent, their number increased by leaps and bounds.

Naturally, they resorted to many tricks and artifices to mislead the enrolling officials into believing that they

43

were ineligible for military duty, either by age or disability. They, and members of their families, became very susceptible to lapses of memory, whereby an eighteen-year-old became a year or two younger, and a man of forty-five suddenly found himself to be forty-six or older.

But the enrollment officers, one for each township, were in most cases personally acquainted with many of the people with whom they had to deal, and refused to be mislead. The enrollments were completed expeditiously, and with very few cases of eligibles having been missed.

With the enrollment lists complete, the next step was the elimination from the rolls of all men who suffered from any obvious disability, such as the loss of an eye, an arm or a leg, lack of teeth, or any other crippling ailment.

This was accomplished by the personal appearance, at the district examining centers, of all claimants of such disabilities, and for many days they flocked to these centers by the hundreds. Varied indeed were the imagined or invented ailments reviewed by the examining board, many with extremely amusing results.

For instance, in the town of Leray (Jefferson County) a man pleaded with enrolling officer Sidney Cooper that he was unfit for the draft. His excuse was: "Some rats dig into mine cistern and died in dare, and I drinks the water and got some poisoned." Mr. Cooper informed him that a change of air and scenery, as afforded by an expense-paid trip south, would do him much good.

One fellow tried to create the impression that he was nearly helpless from weak and crooked legs. His performance was so ludicrous, and the deception so patent, that the examining official decided to have some fun with him.

"Where do you hurt worst when you walk?" he asked, a serious expression on his face.

44

"All over, if you plase sor," replied the man. "Sore as a bile all along from me feet to me body, sure."

"Try to walk quickly across the room," said the doctor.

The man complied, still carrying on the absurd farce. The walk across the room ended near an open door, and he was marched out the door and past a guard. Here he turned about and asked the guard, "Am I eximpt?"

"No," replied the amused guard, "You'll make a great soldier.

At this point the faker gave up the amusing pretense as a failure, and walked away as nimbly as you please. As he went, his ability to use bad and abusive language proved that in this respect, at least, he was neither a cripple nor a beginner.

Another man, far gone with lung disease, appeared at the Watertown draft office for a physical. Of course, he was rejected and in great joy left the examining room, to exclaim to a friend, "Thank the Lord, the doctor says I won't live for six months, and so I'm exempt."

In the October 16, 1862, issue of the *Oswego Weekly Times* appeared this notice, under the heading of "Evasion of the Draft": Persons who cut off their forefingers or pull their front teeth to avoid the draft, will find that they are not exempt. Though they may have unfitted themselves for the infantry, they will still do very well for the artillery, and will be assigned to that branch of the service. For the particularly timid man, the prospect of this change is not an agreeable one."

On the other side of the picture, one man in Watertown had his hair and beard neatly dyed and trimmed, and then presented himself at the enrollment office and declared his age to be forty-four. But the examining surgeon had already been advised of this deception by a

45

watchful special agent, and upon being questioned, the man at last admitted that he was in fact fifty-five years old, but declared that he was perfectly capable of being a soldier. But the examining board, although they appreciated this departure from the usual, reluctantly had to reject the man. His investment in hair dye was a dead loss.

At about this time a "bounty system" was put into effect, designed to induce draft eligible men to enlist, and thus enable the various townships to fill their quotas without actually invoking a draft. A sum of three hundred dollars was paid to each enlistee for a three year enlistment, and many who had hitherto shied away from service now signed up and claimed the local bounty. Many became "bounty jumpers," receiving the sum of money and immediately escaping into Canada, only to reappear at another point, under another name, and repeat the process. It was against this type of gentry that the efficient special agents proved very effective.

An amusing tale involving a Lewis County resident who wished to collect a bounty has been recorded in the *Jefferson County Gazeteer*. This man had previously been rejected because of the total loss of his upper teeth, but that large amount of money (for those days) looked good to him, and he presented himself at the enrollment board in Watertown for enlistment. Here he was accepted and sent to the quartermaster for outfitting.

At this place he unthinkingly took out his new upper plate, and this action was noted by a vigilant special agent, who immediately reported it to the provost marshal.

Fully outfitted, the man was taken before Capt. Emerson, the provost marshal, for "a short drill." In a quick, sharp voice, the captain ordered, "Take off your cap." It was done.

"Front face," snapped the captain, and the man faced to the front, looking every inch a soldier.

"Take out your teeth," came the quick and unexpected order, and amid shouts of laughter, the man without thinking did so. He was immediately sent back to the examining surgeon, teeth in hand, with the order to ask that worthy just how he was to eat hardtack with no upper teeth. The surgeon, having been cleverly deceived, flew into a rage and gave the culprit a real dressing down for the deception; but it is said that he never quite succeeded in living down the false teeth episode.

In a general review of the impact that the Rebellion had on the rural communities of the North, the trials and tribulations of the folks at home must not be forgotten. While the young men were in the South, fighting, suffering, and often dying; the mothers and fathers, brothers and sisters, wives and sweethearts that they had left behind were also suffering untold worries, heartaches, and sorrow.

The often far-between letters from the men at the front were eagerly anticipated, and when received, read and reread. Later, the more impersonal ones were shared with friends and neighbors.

News bulletins posted by most newspapers were eagerly read and widely discussed. News of a northern victory brought great joy and celebration, and these occasions were all too few in the early years of the war. Tidings of defeat for our side were cause for gloom and long faces, even though most folks felt in their hearts that ultimate victory for what they believed to be the right was a foregone conclusion.

Periodical casualty lists, also posted by the newspap-

47

ers from time to time, were anxiously scanned by families who had loved ones in areas of active hostilities. Many were the watchers who turned away from the lists, choked by grief and tears, when a familiar name appeared, knowing that a well-remembered face and figure had disappeared forever from their usual haunts. And transversely, many were the sighs of relief when an entire list of killed and wounded was read through without having a certain name appear.

Although many families had very little in the way of luxuries themselves, most of them managed by skimping and saving to put together packages of hard-to-get articles to send to their man at the front. Of course, there were no Red Cross or Y.M.C.A. services in those days, but the women of the communities organized various "Soldiers' Aid Societies" and sent packets of food and clothing to the men in the south. However, transportation facilities were so slow that most food items spoiled before they reached the soldiers.

In an old dairy kept by Mrs. Simon Pruyn, whose son Wellington Howard Pruyn, although only sixteen years of age, ran away from home and enlisted in the cavalry, is found the following entry under the date of April 18, 1864: "Packed a box of eatables for Wellington consisting of eggs, ham, dried beef, dried apples, green apples, dried berries, ketchup, horseradish, sugar, butter, cheese, pepper, tobacco and cigars. Box and all weighed 85 pounds." In a later entry she wrote: "Went up to the village (Sandy Creek) to a soldiers' aid society meeting. Carried two shirts, one wrapper, some dried apples, berries, and currants."

The counties of Jefferson, Lewis, and Oswego, whose environs embrace most of the Tug Hill plateau, may well be proud of the manner in which they gave of their sons

48

in the Great War. But in this respect Oswego County can be especially proud. With a population of 75,600 in 1860, she sent eleven thousand men into the service, or nearly fifteen per cent of her people. It has been stated that Oswego County furnished more men for the war in proportion to its population than any other county in the whole United States.

THE STRONG MAN
OF MONTAGUE

Probably every chronicler of backwoods history has at some time come across stories concerning the exploits of famous strong men. Certainly not all of these are true. Many of them escape the bounds of probability, some of them even the bounds of possibility. But once in a while one hears accounts of the doings of men whose existence and deeds are substantiated by actual and irrefutable proof, and in this category belongs the story of Joseph Laits.

Joe was born and brought up on a farm in the then prosperous town of Montague, high on the eastern slope of Tug Hill in Lewis County. Here the winters were extremely rigorous, with deep snows and roaring blizzards, and lasted from November until April.

While Joe was still very young, his father volunteered for service with the Union army during the Civil War, or Rebellion, as it was then known. He and several other settlers walked to Sackets Harbor, where they were organized for shipment to the front. For the next few years, the boy's mother had to carry on the task of fending off starvation from a large family, and getting them through the long and savage winters.

Once a month, weather and the vagaries of war permitting, the father's army check came to the postoffice in Lowville, and at these times the mother would trudge the

51

many miles to town to exchange it for flour and other staple provisions. These she would carry home on her back, arriving long after dark during the winter months. In bad weather Joe's brother John, who was the oldest of the family, would start out in the afternoon to meet his mother and help carry the groceries home. During these times the eldest girl in the family, who was nine or ten, took charge of the other children, kept the fires going, and had a pot of hot tea ready for her mother and brother when they arrived.

Joe spent much of his adult life on another farm a few miles from the old homestead in Montague. Here, by dint of unrelenting labor, he managed to wrest from the stony and unfriendly soil a living for himself and family. Now and then he would work for a spell in a lumber camp or sawmill, and sometimes in the spring seasons he hired out as a log driver on the riotous Salmon, Mad, and Deer Rivers; in this way supplementing the family income to a considerable extent. In those days jobs were few and far between, and a man must make a dollar whenever and however he could.

Tall, broad and raw-boned, Joe had the muscles to match his build, and really looked the part of a strongman. And proof that this appearance was no deception began to make itself evident early in his young manhood. While he was no show-off, tales of the prodigious strength that he sometimes used in performing his everyday duties began to travel throughout the territory. Some folks, perhaps a little envious, said that he used more strength than common sense. However this may have been, ample proof exists that he possessed plenty of both.

Of a somewhat mild and peaceful nature, Mr. Laits never gained the fame as a rough-and-tumble fighter that he might have, had he been of a more pugnacious make-

A sample of Tug Hill deer. Gentleman at right is author's father. Gentleman at left is author at six years of age.

Log scaling at the turn of the century.

John Bush and his wife, Jane. It was Mr. Bush who captured yearling bear alive. Picture taken soon after this event.

Sawmill at Swancott's Mills, early 1900's

Crew on the mill pond.

A big load of logs ready to leave Tug Hill. Note the fringe mittens worn by teamster.

Camp and woods crew of the Blount Lumber Company, 1920. White-haired gentleman in center is foreman Thomas Brennan.

Part of group of State Forestry College students employed by the Blount Lumber Company in their first reforestation project, 1916.

A typical lumbercamp layout.

Osceola camp of the Harden Lumber Company, 1921. Left to right: Fred Fox, D. Ammon, Mrs. Gregory (cook), J. Masterson, Clarence C. Harden.

Barn at Harden Lumber Company camp

Top grade Tug Hill logs.

up. Even in the uproarious lumbering towns of that area and era, he would never engage in a fight if it were possible to avoid it. And few bullies, no matter how deep in their cups they might be, ever cared to deliberately precipitate an encounter with a man of such impressive build and reputation. But in the few instances where it was necessary for him to fight, witnesses said that the ease with which he inflicted destruction on his assailants was a beautiful thing to see.

However, as the years went by, his strength remained his chief claim to fame. Many were the tales of his amazing feats, and while most of these have been lost in the limbo of intervening time, some still persist to this day. The author's own father, who knew Mr. Laits in the 1890's, after he had reached quite an advanced age, has told many times of one of these feats which he witnessed. It happened while he, as a young man, was working in a sawmill at Hooker, near where Mr. Laits lived.

It seems that the strong-man had a white ash log which he figured was straight-grained enough to be sawed into wagon-tongue material. But the log, which was ten feet in length and something over a foot in diameter on the butt end, was in the woods a mile from the mill; and in a difficult place to get with a horse. So instead of going to the trouble of cutting a skidding trail, Joe simply put the log on his shoulder and carried it to the mill; where he upended it onto the rollway with a shrug of his muscular torso.

Now this in itself is no mean task, when one considers that such a log weighs several hundred pounds. But viewed in the light of some of his other exploits, it is not so difficult to believe.

An account of one of the fights in which Mr. Laits was involved was related to the writer by a Mr. James A.

53

Ward of Watertown, who was a nephew of his. The tale was told to Mr. Ward by his mother, who was a sister of the strong-man and a witness of the event.

It seems that the lady, another younger sister, and their brother, Joe, were seated in the dining room of the old Strife House in Lowville, quietly having their dinner, when in rushed a greatly excited acquaintance.

"Joe, you've got to come quick," the man shouted. " . . . (he named a fellow with whom they were all acquainted) is in the saloon in a fight with five half-breed Indians. He's getting beat up real bad. You've got to come and stop it before they kill him."

Joe pushed back his chair and rose to his feet. "Did he start it?" he asked, knowing full well that the fellow had a habit of starting trouble.

"No," said the informer, "the Indians picked on him."

On receiving this information Joe picked up his hat, and in spite of the protests of his two sisters, followed the man a short distance down the street to the saloon, from which could now be heard the uproar from the melee within. The sisters, of course, remained at the Strife House but kept their attention fixed on the saloon.

In a moment there was a shattering of glass, and an Indian came sailing out through a front window of the saloon, to sprawl in the mud of the street. He was followed by another, and at intervals, the other three, until all five were piled up in a badly mauled and scarcely conscious heap.

After a few moments Joe came through the door of the saloon, half carrying and half supporting the man who had been set upon by the Indians. Setting him down in a chair on the veranda and leaving him there in the care of his friends, Joe turned back toward the hotel,

54

wiping his huge hands on his trouser legs. There, after rejoining his sisters, he nonchalantly finished his dinner, hardly mentioning the fight from which he had received very little noticeable damage.

But other witnesses to the affair told afterward that no one else had dared take the white man's part against the drunken Indians, and that Joe had thrown them out single-handed as fast as he could get to them.

In those days when physical prowess was valued so highly, many tests of strength were devised and practiced wherever a group of men happened to congregate for a few idle moments. Among these were twisting the broomstick, weight lifting, Indian wrestling, and wrist-twisting.

Joe Laits is said to have had very little liking for these show-off tactics, but because of his strength was always getting roped into them. And also mainly because of his strength, he became quite adept and gained fame in these sports, especially wrist-twisting.

While he never took much pride in or bragged about his ability in this respect, his attitude was not shared by many another strong man throughout the Tug Hill country. Many of these fellows were considered local champions at wrist-twisting, and would walk miles to pit their strength and skill against that of another champion. Sometimes public matches were arranged between two champions, with a great deal of side betting on the results; but oftentimes a man would travel a long distance to challenge another to a private contest, simply because his pride would not let him rest until he knew for sure which was the better man.

One of these cocky fellows walked all the way from Rodman to Montague one day, in quest of such a contest with Joe. Not knowing exactly where Joe lived, he stopped to inquire from a burly looking stranger who was splitting fence rails alongside the road.

"Why yes, I know Joe Laits," said the man in answer to the query. "Lives right up the road a piece, in that there house." Picking up a twelve-foot rail by the end, he pointed it with one hand up the road toward a farm a short distance away.

The eyes of the Rodman champion fairly bugged from his head at this display of muscular power. Then suddenly a faint suspicion began to take form in his mind.

"Say friend," he remarked admiringly, "you're a pretty strong man. Mind telling me your name?"

"Why no, sir," said Joe politely, "I'd as lief tell you, seein's you asked me. Name's Joe Laits."

The Rodman man turned in his tracks and started back the way he had come, a sheepish grin on his face.

"Wait sir," called Joe. "You ain't told me yet who you might be."

"Just call me a damn fool that walked all the way from Rodman to twist your wrist," the man called back over his shoulder.

Probably the most told and best remembered tale concerning Joe Laits, and the one that provoked the most amusement, concerned his experience with an ox on his farm up in Montague. The writer thinks that it also best illustrates his sense of humor and direct logic.

As the story goes, he had a team of mammoth oxen which he used in cultivation of the farm, as well as for skidding logs and clearing land. One spring, when the plowing was all done except for a few furrows down the side of one field, one of the oxen had the lack of consideration to up and die.

Now this turn of affairs was almost as tragic for Joe

56

as for the ox. At this busy time of the year it was well nigh impossible to borrow or hire an animal, and a habitual shortage of cash made purchasing a replacement just as prohibitive. But the spring's work had to go on if there was to be a crop to harvest the next fall. How to get the rest of the plowing done was a problem.

After giving the matter a good deal of thought, Joe hit upon a plan which he thought might work. He talked it over with his wife, who tried to dissuade him, but in spite of this he decided to give it a try anyway.

Placing the yoke on the remaining ox, he hitched it to the plow. Then poking his own head through the bow at the other end of the yoke, and settling his powerful shoulders against the hoop, he and the ox set off down the field. Mrs. Laits followed behind, guiding the plow as best she could in the stony soil.

Joe said afterward that he was pulling his share of the plow alright, and that everything would have been fine if the consarned ox hadn't suddenly started getting ideas of his own. He hadn't cared much for the unusual proceedings from the start, and all at once he decided that he wasn't going to put up with them any longer. With a suddenness surprising in so cumbersome a beast, he put his tail over his back, let out a bellow, and set off crosslots. Behind him he dragged the wildly struggling Joe, the wildly bounding plow, and the wildly screaming woman.

Around and around they went, making two or three circuits of the field before some men who were passing on the road finally came to the rescue, and after a merry chase succeeded in herding the whole kit and kaboodle into the corner of a stone fence.

There they turned their attention to trying to extricate Joe from the yoke, unhurt but considerably winded.

57

And right then he displayed a canny sense of logic by the remark that has caused so much amusement down through the intervening years.

"Never mind me," panted Joe. "Unhook the danged ox . . . I'll stand."

GREENBOROUGH,
A LOST COMMUNITY

Scattered between the Tug Hill area and the region that lies between the Hill and Lake Ontario, are the sites of many little hamlets and villages. Once thriving and prosperous communities, these little places, whose names once were known for miles around, have become scarcely more than memories in the rush of present-day living.

Some of them may still be found on antique maps, but in most instances the terrain itself yields only a very few physical traces of their existence. A group of overgrown cellar holes here; the rotting remnants of a mill-dam there; these are about all that remain to remind one of the activity and industry that once flourished there.

The causes of the demise and eventual extinction of these erstwhile villages were many and varied. Unlike the ancient cities of Pompeii and Carthage, their ends came about not as the result of some phenomenal upheaval of nature or the activities of a savage enemy. Rather, they were hastened by the change and modernization of the very economic system that first brought them into being.

The diminishing of a certain road's importance as a main artery of travel; lessening of the necessity of streams as a source of power; failure of the water-power itself due to lumbered-off watersheds; concentration of the population in towns served by railroads; all these and more contributed their share toward the disappearance of the many small hamlets that used to dot the countryside.

A perfect example of this is the complete disappearance of the village once known as Greenborough. Today the name roughly applies to a general territory covering half a township, but few indeed are the remaining persons who remember the site of the actual settlement.

Situated in the extreme northern end of Redfield Township and about halfway between Lorraine and Redfield Square, Greenborough straddled the old Military Highway that ran from Rome to Sackett's Harbor, just at the point where it was crossed by Cottrell Creek (west branch of Salmon River). This road was for many years the main artery of travel between the Mohawk country and northern New York, and as such was an important stage and freight route.

At the time of its heyday, just before the turn of the century, Greenborough could boast of quite a bit of industry. The fast-flowing waters of the creek furnished power for several booming enterprises; among them a sawmill, a butter-tub factory, a plate factory, two box factories, and a stave-mill. Also located here were a store, schoolhouse, blacksmith shop, cheese-factory, several dwellings, and the famous old Cottrell Hotel, well-known for many years as a famous tavern and stage-stop. The community had its own post-office, the mail being delivered to it twice a week from the railroad at Lacona. While it had no church of its own, the village was served by St. Joseph's Catholic Church one mile north toward Lorraine, and Union Church, one mile south toward Redfield. Of these, only the latter now remains.

North of the village, and extending along the west side of the road to its junction with the Smartville Road, was a long, narrow area known as The Commons. Most of this tract was fenced in and served as a common grazing ground for sheep, horses, and young stock. But part of it was always kept secure against the inroads of these animals, for here grew thousands of huckleberry bushes which in summer were loaded with luscious fruit that was always free for the picking. At the northern end, near the Catholic Church, was a beautiful spruce grove in which were picnic grounds, benches, and a pavilion in which could be held parties and dances. In summer months this served as a kind of social center for the surrounding territory, which boasted many large and productive farms and was quite thickly populated by large families. Many a gay time is said to have been had there.

An interesting tale is told of how one prominent citizen tried to better the community, only to have the plan backfire on him. This gentleman was named Webb, his first name being probably Josiah, and he was one of the first settlers in the neighborhood and founder of the original inn known later as the Cottrell Hotel.

As the community grew, Mr. Webb noted the importance of waterpower as an inducement to more settlers and more industry. What, he wondered, would be the result if the creek carried two or three times the volume of water than it did now? The more he thought about it the more it intrigued him, and no doubt this well-meaning but sadly misguided gentleman had rosy visions of what the future held for the community as he set about seeing what could be done about it.

Being very well acquainted with the surrounding terrain, Mr. Webb knew of a spot made to order for his purpose. High up toward the crest of Tug Hill, Mad River, which is really the main branch of the Salmon, swings in a huge loop from north to west to south; this being known as the Big Bend. Now at the point where this loop is completed, the southward trend is accomplished by an abrupt and tumultous elbow-bend; and right here the head-waters of Cottrell Creek, on which Greenborough was located, are only a short quarter mile away, separated by only a low ridge from the river that it joined many miles below.

As Mr. Webb looked the locality over, he knew that this was the spot. A wide ditch dug through the separating ridge just where the turn began, with only a few feet of solid ground left intact . . . a few huge trees dropped into the river just below the ditch's mouth to create a dam and turn the current . . . a good-sized charge of dynamite to remove the last barrier of solid earth, just before a freshet. These would accomplish the transformation without too great an expense.

During the dry season that summer the old schemer hired a couple of teams of oxen, equipped them with plows, scrapers, and drivers, and disappeared into the woods for a few weeks. Just how he planned to get away with the scheme has not been recorded. The secrecy with which the whole affair was conducted seems to indicate that he had a good idea that altering the course of a river was not exactly lawful. But perhaps he thought that, once the change was effected, the racing waters would soon erase all signs of tampering and the whole thing would be blamed to a quirk of nature.

Anyway, he dug his ditch, standing the entire expense himself. The dynamite was carted in and stored ready for instant use. Everything was in readiness for the first fall rains, when a blast would send Mad River roaring down the new channel and transform Greenborough into a metropolis.

Nobody knows for sure just how the secret leaked

62

out. Perhaps the inhabitants of Littlejohn, a community a few miles down the river from the project and also dependent upon its water-power, may have had something to do with it. However it was, the state deparment controlling such matters learned of the scheme, disapproved of the whole proceedings, and slapped a restraining order on the instigator.

The dynamite blast was never set off and Mad River still flows in its natural course. But Webb's Ditch remained in evidence for a good many years, and the author can remember having traces of it pointed out to him by his father many years ago.

Like many another rural region, Greenborough had its classic ghost story. During the 1880's a weathered human skeleton was discovered wedged into a stone culvert which passed beneath the Old State Road in a slight depression about three miles south, or toward Redfield. These remains were of an adult male of slight stature, and were thought to be those of a Jewish pack-peddler who had mysteriously disappeared in the general area a couple of years before.

Rumor had it that the man had stopped to spend the night at a local farmhouse and had been murdered for the money and wares that he carried. Evidence of foul play must have been very sketchy, however, for no action in the matter was ever taken by the authorities.

However, local legend has it that the man's spirit must have decided to take vengeance into its own nebulous hands, for soon afterward reports began to circulate of several persons, some of them of unimpeachable integrity, having encountered the shadowy specter of a pack-peddler, pack and all, stalking the roads and fields near the culvert where the skeleton was discovered. Evidently he was seeking for his murderer, for he never molested any of the folks who saw him; except, perhaps, for causing them to suffer a shock from which they did not recover for many a day.

The place became known as "Dead Man's Hollow" and for many years was universally dreaded by young and old alike; especially the former, who could rarely be persuaded to pass the spot after the evening shadows began to fall, except as a member of a large group.

The gradual downfall and disappearance of Greenborough came about in the usual way. The old Military Highway was replaced by newer and shorter thoroughfares, and lost its importance as a stage and freight route, the railroads usurping both the freight and the travelers. Steam and gasoline power nullified the necessity of water-power, and industries moved away to more readily accessible sites. Old settlers died off, and the young people drifted away to the cities with their expanding factories and prosperous jobs, or to more promising farming regions. Timber that had been grist for the mills was depleted.

The last industry to close its doors was a box-factory, this having been gone for a good fifty years. The very last building to succumb was, ironically, almost the first to have been built. This was the old Cottrel Hotel, long before converted to dwelling apartments, which was torn down in the late 1930's.

Almost the entire site of the settlement, the Commons, and most of the surrounding farms have been reforested and are now well grown up to trees.

Nowadays, motorists traveling the Old Military Road, which is now fine macadam and designated on the maps as N. Y. Route 285, flash heedlessly through the valley where never a last building is left standing to mark the spot once occupied by the prosperous and bustling hamlet of Greenborough.

64

ON TUG HILL
LUMBERING

Because of its high altitude, with attendant late frosts in the spring and early frosts in the fall, the Tug Hill plateau as a whole has never been ideally suited for agriculture, although some good farms do flourish within its scope. But lumbering has played, and in some sections still does play, a very important part in its development and economic welfare.

When the first white settlers began to trickle into the area in the early 1800's, the whole region was virtually buried in verdant, untouched forests. Towering spruce and hemlocks, three and four feet through at the base, and with here and there a stand of native pine interspersed, vied with various deciduous trees such as maple, ash, beech, and red birch for space and sunlight. Only the red men and the beasts that they pursued had ever roamed the dim fastnesses, and none of the forest giants had ever been disturbed by axe or saw.

But to the white settlers these forests were a nuisance rather than a blessing. Of course, clearings had to be slashed in the dense growth so that they might cultivate the meager crops that insured at least a precarious living during the long, hard winters. Thus began the gradual demise of that beautiful camouflage with which nature had disguised the rock-ribbed maze that comprises the Tug Hill plateau.

The eventual disappearance of the original forests can be separated into two distinct eras: that of simple timber eradication, and that of lumbering proper. As has been said, the first began with the clearing of farm sites. Thousands of beautiful trees were ruthlessly cut down, chopped into lengths convenient for piling, and burned to get them out of the way. The only usable by-product from these was the ashes that helped to enrich the land.

Soon after this the demand for hemlock bark by the numerous tanneries that sprang up brought on the era of the bark peelers. Countless numbers of giant hemlocks were cut down, and after the bark was stripped from them they were left to rot, thus wasting millions of board feet of lumber. Only the bark was used. This was ground fine and utilized in the tanning of hides for the production of leather.

Up to this point and far beyond, hardwood trees such as oak, maple, birch, beech, and ash were largely ignored as a source of lumber. A small percentage was cut for firewood, but otherwise little use was found for them.

The period of proper lumbering in the region could be said to have begun in the last half of the nineteenth century. Various lumbering companies sprang up, or migrated from other states, notably Pennsylvania, and the actual harvesting of the rich timber resources began.

In 1867, a man named David Swancott moved into the southeast side of the Tug Hill area, about twenty miles north of Rome. Here, on Fish Creek, he built a dam and established a water-powered sawmill, around which a sizeable settlement known as Swancott's Mills quickly grew up.

At this place Mr. Swancott developed a diversified manufacturing enterprise. Besides lumber, he produced broom handles which supplied a broom factory in Amsterdam, and he also operated a plant which produced oars and paddles. The latter activity being entirely new,

66

paddle finishers were practically non-existent in the area, so he imported a few from various southern states. The sawmill also put out crossties for use by the railroads in expanding their ever-growing systems.

Swancott's Mills boasted, besides these manufactories, a boarding house, schoolhouse, general store, dance hall, and several houses owned by the company for the use of married employees. In its heyday the place even had its own baseball team that used to play in competition with other local teams. Some sixty or more men were employed there, as well as seventy-five teams of horses for skidding and hauling logs.

The businesses were carried on for many years, finally succumbing to the lack of readily available raw materials, as did many others. The tract of land, including the site of the former settlement, was purchased about 1920 by the Gould Paper Company.

Another among the first of these lumbering interests was an outfit organized and operated by a man named Ebenezer Hooker. His scene of operation was high up on the east flank of the Hill, in what is now known as Montague, Lewis County. Here Mr. Hooker, a part-time minister with a good deal of lumbering know-how, erected a large dam and sawmill on Mad River, a few miles below its source. A thriving little settlement grew up around the enterprise, taking the name of Hooker in honor of its founder. The area still bears that name, although nothing remains there now but a few hunting camps.

Timber for the Hooker mill came mostly from the headwaters of Mad River, because of the logical fact that timber could be floated downstream but not up, and consisted almost entirely of spruce, hemlock, and pine. The operation went on for many years, during the 80's and

90's, but finally had to be abandoned for lack of suitable timber.

During this period, other lumbering enterprises had pushed their way in from the eastern and northern sides of the Hill. Logs were cut and floated down the Black and Deer Rivers to various mills at Glenfield, Lowville, Carthage, and Copenhagen. It was at this time that log driving, practiced for years in other states, began to assume the importance in the area that it was to gain in later years. The tumultous, snow-fed streams that roared down from the Hill in early spring converted the larger rivers into waterways ideal for this purpose.

Simultaneously, the area was also introduced to a breed of lumberjack previously unknown thereabouts: the log-driver. The increase of lumbering operations had triggered an influx of woodsmen from other regions, especially French-Canadians from lower Ontario and Quebec. Among them were men who knew all the ins and outs of river-driving, and these individuals introduced their own methods and practices. These were soon picked up by others and modified to fit the conditions existing along the various streams.

But with them also came the skill, the daring, the devil-may-care spirit that enabled them to survive countless dangers and hardships, and this also was quickly emulated by the natives. With scarcely a second thought they encountered and overcame conditions that would have killed lesser men: living for days on end in clothing that was never dry, wading through deep snow along stream banks, working endless hours each day and sleeping a few hours at night in sodden blankets inside hastily constructed brush shelters, often in freezing weather. Rough but wholesome food was furnished by a cook who followed the drive in a scow, always provided, of course, that he could keep up with the logs. Sometimes the cook went ahead of the drive, setting up camp where the drivers could snatch a hasty meal as they went by. But this was considered a risky business and was not much resorted to.

Of course, not all of them escaped unscathed. Danger in many forms was always present. Legs and arms were broken, bumps and bruises were plentiful. Some few were overwhelmed and crushed by breaking log jams. Ebenezer Hooker's eldest son slipped between the closely packed logs in the holding pond at the Hooker mill and, being unable to surface, quickly drowned.

But there were light moments also. Many of these rough lumberjacks, especially the French-Canadians, had beautiful singing voices that they liked to exercise, and many times the woods along the rivers rang with chantys and folksongs. And at the end of the drive there was always the trip into a nearby village or town, with wages in their pockets and a hunger for excitement in their hearts.

Many tales have been told and many legends have sprung up concerning these forays into the lumbering towns. If the word went out, "The drivers are coming with chips in their pockets," the business people breathed easier, especially the saloon-keepers. For this meant that the river-men were peaceable, and meant no mischief. The chips that they carried in their pockets were evidence of that. These were placed on the bottoms of their calked shoes before they entered a building, thus rendering the sharp spikes incapable of mutilating and shredding the floors.

But if the warning came that the drivers were on the way with no chips in their pockets, or if a gang for some reason started to "shed their chips," it always meant to prepare for trouble. The river-jacks were in a cantankerous mood and anything could happen. Usually it did. Many were the vicious brawls that erupted suddenly and savagely, brought on by a careless word or action after the consumption of about just so much "alky" or red-eye liquor had set tempers aflame.

In these "affairs of honor" no mercy was shown or asked. Weapons were confined to whatever a man could lay his hands on, and the fight usually went on until one combatant was rendered totally incapable of defending himself, and his opponent was dragged away by the crowd of watchers. Many a saloon was virtually torn apart in these affairs; and many a lumberjack carried to his grave facial decorations acquired through forceful contact with a calked shoe or a set of brass knuckles.

In time many places of business in the lumbering towns adapted the practice of keeping beside their doors a pile of small, soft pine boards, about six inches square and one-half inch thick. These were supposed to be used in place of the proverbial chips, and when utilized by a cooperative gang of lumberjacks, set up a fearful clatter as the men moved about, but saved many a floor from becoming ruined by the sharp calks.

Along in the last decade of the 1800's, two new lumbering enterprises were established on the western side of the Hill. The first of these was situated a few miles below where Mad River straightens out in a southerly course after making the "Big Bend," at a point where the road from Greenborough to Montague later went up over the Hill. A large sawmill was erected there with a huge timber dam that backed the water up the river for over a mile. This became known as Littlejohn Settlement, named after its founder, and later came to boast several houses, a store, a boarding house, and even a school.

The other, situated about five miles farther downstream, became known as Otto Mills, and also boasted a large mill and dam. Both of these mills were water-powered, and supplying the huge amounts of timber required to supply their whirling saws did much toward decimating the forests on the western slopes of the plateau.

Mr. John Hogan, a gentleman now in his seventies, and who has followed the lumbering industry all of his life, relates how his father used to have charge of releasing the impounded water from the Otto Mills dam for the start of the spring drive. The elder Mr. Hogan would be at the dam and open the gates at one o'clock in the morning of the appointed day; then with a good driving horse would beat the "swash," or head of water, into Redfield several miles downstream. Here the drivers would be assembled waiting for the swash to start the logs moving, and Mr. Hogan would join them for the drive downriver to a sawmill located near Altmar, on what had by this time become Salmon River. The mill used to stand about where a large hydro-electric dam is now backing the water up the river for miles.

These operations were all consummated on the east side of Mad River. A few good stands of softwood still remained in the territory west of the river, and these were not disturbed until during the year of World War II when George Colvin lumbered off this area and took the good hardwood as well as the softwood.

Not much attention was paid to the heavy stands of hardwoods until the early 1900's. At this time a new concern, the Blount Lumber Company, was formed by George R. Blount at Lacona. Mr. Blount was one of the first to realize the potential value of the beech, birch, maple, and cherry that grew so abundantly throughout

71

the region, and purchased large tracts of land in the Boylston, Redfield, and Osceola areas, as well as around Williamstown and Parish.

Up until this time Mr. Blount had limited his operations to a small shop in Lacona where he manufactured chair rockers, but now he began to establish lumber-camps on his holdings and started to harvest the large amounts of hardwood timber available. A quite large, steam-powered sawmill was built in Boylston on the west branch of Salmon River, known locally as Cottrell Creek, and here sawing operations were carried on for several years. The huge pile of sawdust that was then a useless by-product of these operations, can yet be seen, still as high and wide as a fair-sized hill, although greatly shrunken from its original size.

The lumber thus obtained was transported to Lacona, where the Blount enterprises built and operated a large hardwood flooring plant, complete with its own dry-kilns and storage sheds. Later, a very modern and efficient sawmill was also erected adjacent to the flooring plant, and here hundreds of thousands of board feet of lumber were produced every year.

At first, all of the hauling, both of logs and lumber, was done by horse-power. But Mr. Blount at a very early date realized that this method was fast becoming outmoded, and was the first to adopt the caterpillar tread vehicle method of transportation. His first tractors were Holt half-tracks and Linn tractors with sleigh runners ahead for steering, in place of wheels. This mode of hauling demanded a better type of hauling road than previously, and kept a gang of "road-monkeys" busy all winter with sprinklers, hardening the tracks. But it also enabled the movement of ten times the volume of timber in much less time. It was something of a sight to see one of these vehicles, itself carrying a full load and hauling five to eight sleigh-loads behind, making its bellowing way through the woods.

Several of these super hauling roads were constructed, ending in landing places on good roads, where, when spring came, the logs were placed on trucks and transported to the big mill at Lacona. One of the larger "landings" was situated at Smartville, and through this millions of feet of hardwood found its way down from the forests of Boylston, Redfield, and Osceola.

The Blount enterprises also established other camps in the Williamstown-Parish-West Amboy areas, with extensive operations around Panther Lake. Later, when the timber supply began to dwindle, the company found it more profitable to let out contracts for cutting and hauling to smaller, individual operators, rather than to maintain their own camps.

The big mill at Lacona continued to operate until after World War II, when both it and the flooring plant were abandoned. The Blount Lumber Company still does a flourishing business, but now as a manufacturer of windows, doors, and millwork products. Most of their lumber now comes from the pine and fir forests of the western states.

The founder of the company, George R. Blount, was one of the first pioneers of reforestation in this part of the state. Mr. Blount quickly realized that the native forests were not inexhaustible, and that in order to continue to reap, one must also plant. His tree planting operations began as early as 1916, and continued, much against the near-sighted wishes of many of the residents of the region, for the remainder of his life.

The Harden Furniture Company of McConnellsville near Camden carried on logging operations during the period 1914-1923 from their forest holdings near Osceola to supply their furniture plant with high grade birch and maple. They are now manufacturing solid cherry furniture for their markets throughout the nation but purchase their log supply from a great variety of places.

During the first two decades of the present century the adoption by the railroads of the use of hardwood cross-ties placed an added demand on the supply of hardwood timber. Small concerns equipped with light, portable "tie mills" went into operation throughout the Tug Hill region. These harvested timber for railroad ties that would not have been touched by former operators, and countless thousands of these eight and a half foot timbers were sent down out of the forests to shipping points on the railroad. From there they were shipped to the New York Central's tie plant near Rome, where they were virtually cooked in creosote and sent to all parts of the railroad's vast network.

It was during this period that the Nobles brothers, Earl and Arthur, began operations in the woods of Boylston and Redfield, with their mill situated in the former locality. Unlike most of the other small operators, their enterprise continued to grow to reach sizeable proportions, and went on until Arthur was killed by a load of logs that broke its bindings and overwhelmed him. After that Earl carried on the business alone for several years, pausing for a while during World War II to act as a timber and lumber inspector for the government.

Another of the mill operators who started small and went on to achieve considerable stature and importance was Dean Williams of Redfield. Mr. Williams carried on a profitable and extensive business in that village for many years, furnishing employment for many lumbermen in his woods and mill projects.

74

It was during this era that the last remaining stands of "green timber," or virgin forests high up on the Hill began to succumb. For years the Gould Paper Company at Lyons Falls had owned and jealously guarded these last stands of spruce and hemlock for use in time of a national emergency or some other real need. But at last the ever-increasing demands for more and more newsprint forced them to use the pulpwood resource from their Tug Hill tract.

The McCarthy brothers, Bill, Jim and Pat, contracted for the removal of much of this timber, and operated in this area for several years. To facilitate the delivery of this vast amount of pulpwood, the Glenfield and Western Railroad ran a spur line up onto the Hill from the Black River valley, on the east side. This also operated for several years.

Along in the late 1930's the Gould Paper Company decided that the time was again ripe for harvesting the pulpwood on the upper reaches of Fish Creek and Roaring Brook. Elmer Bernier was the jobber on this project, with Joe Morin acting as his woods and river foreman. Mr. Bernier established two large camps, one near the jack-works on Fish Creek, the other a few miles farther up into the woods.

During the regular cutting and peeling season, from May until August, thousands of cords of mature spruce were cut and stripped of bark. The Gould Paper Company had for years practiced a program of selective cutting, taking no trees under ten inches in diameter at the stump. The ten-inch minimum insured another cut in the same area in roughly thirty years. However, on this job this rule could largely be dispensed with, as most of the timber was well over that size.

In late summer skidding teams were brought in and

75

the logs were skidded to big skidways along the hauling roads. They were hauled by Linn tractors in winter on well-iced roads to Roaring Brook and Fish Creek for the spring log drive.

With the coming of spring and the release of tremendous amount of snow-water, the usually placid streams became raging torrents. Joe Morin and his men launched the waiting logs and conducted a very successful drive to the jack-works on Fish Creek. Here they were lifted by mechanical means up an inclined ramp and loaded on trucks, which took them to the big paper mill at Lyons Falls. When Elmer Bernier completed this operation on Fish Creek, John Hogan became logging superintendent for the Gould Paper Company in operations near Osceola.

The Adirondack Core and Plug Company of Carthage had extensive hardwood operations on the east side of Tug Hill, west of Houseville. They used the former Glenfield and Western Railroad bed as a truck road. Jack Hogan of Osceola and Joe McDermitt of Port Leyden were the logging operators.

George Colvin was one of the big-time operators in the area, and a native son, having been born and brought up near North Osceola. Here he entered into the lumbering business at an early age, his first jobs being in partnership with his father and his uncle, William Colvin. As time went by, his excellent woods knowledge, his skill at managing logging operations, and his employment of advanced and labor-saving methods, enabled him to take on larger and larger jobs. One of his labor-saving systems, evidence of which may still be seen, was the practice of using the beds of small streams as routes for hauling roads. This insured moderate grades and eliminated a great deal of road building.

Mr. Colvin operated extensively all through the Adirondacks, as well as on Tug Hill. Probably he harvested as much or more timber from the Hill as any other jobber, alive or dead.

Joe Kwasniewski of West Leyden organized the J and C Lumber Company in 1948 and built a softwood mill there. A major project in 1951 was the fallen timber from the big blowdown in November, 1950.

The company built a new modern hardwood mill near Swancott's Mills in 1960 and now operates on lands of the Gould Paper Company, which is now part of the far-flung Georgia-Pacific Company program.

The highest annual cut has been 4,000,000 feet of choice hardwood, especially yellow birch, which has been sold in markets mostly on the east coast.

The last of the great, original, virgin forests of the Tug Hill plateau have passed. True, some lumbering operations are still carried on there, especially since the development of wood processing methods to their present level. What is known as "hardwood pulpwood" is now harvested, thus utilizing much hitherto valueless timber.

Operational procedures have, of course, changed completely. Gone are the lumber camps; the log drives with their singing, fighting, river-jacks; the crosscut saw; the bark spud; calked shoes and the double-bitted axe. The bulldozer and chainsaw have come into their own.

A lumbering outfit now goes into an area with their sophisticated machinery, either on an established road or one bulldozed for the purpose. Whenever a good stand of timber is found, a side road is bulldozed for a short distance into it, until a good spot for a power skidder can be provided. The trees are then cut down, trimmed and cut off at the topmost redeemable extremity; the

77

cable and tongs from the power skidder are then brought
in and attached, and away goes the whole tree to the
loading area.

Here it is chainsawed into the desired lengths, loaded
by a power loader onto trucks, and is on its way to whichever mill is destined to receive it. Whenever the timber
within easy reach of the skidder has been exhausted,
the outfit moves on to a new location, and the whole
process is repeated.

Of course, this is progress; but progress at the cost
of the picturesqueness, the romanticism, the colorfulness
that once characterized old-time lumbering. Fortunate
indeed are the few of us who have seen, and can still remember, even the later of these halcyon days.

THE LUMBERJACKS' ALPHABET

A is for axes, we very well know,
And B is for boys who can use them also,
C is for chopping, the first to begin,
And D is for danger we often are in.

Chorus

So merry, so merry, so merry are we,
No mortals on earth are as happy as we,
Hi derry, ho derry, hi derry down,
Give shanty boys grog and there's nothing goes wrong.

E is for echoes, that through the woods rang,
F is for foreman who followed his gang,
G is for grindstone, so round and so swift,
And H is for handle, we all have to twist.

I is for ice, on rivers and ponds,
J is for jacknife, that each of us owns,
K is for keen, our axes to keep,
And L is for lice, that keeps us from sleep.

M is for moss that we stick in our camps,
N is for needle that mendeth our pants,
O is for owl, that hooted at night,
And P is for pine, that always falls right.

Q is for quarrels we never allow,
R is for river, that takes our logs down,
S is for sleds, so stout and so strong,
And T is for teams that haul them along.

U is the use that we put our teams to,
V is for valley we haul our logs through,
W is the woods we leave in the spring,
And now you have heard all I'm going to sing.

THE SPRUCE-GUMMERS
OF TUG HILL

Away back in the old days, seventy-five or eighty years ago, long before the general exodus from the backwoods sections of New York State, spruce gum gathering was one of the most profitable, as well as one of the most interesting and picturesque winter occupations of the semi-wilderness people. In fact, it was often the only source of ready money available between late fall and early spring.

In those days nearly every family in these regions was a self-supporting, substantial little community all by itself. They were trained from childhood to do things for themselves, just as, lamentably, many children today are encouraged to throw all their difficult tasks and responsibilities onto the shoulders of others. But, of course, this was long before the day of the welfare state. A person sank or swam by his own efforts and ingenuity, and many would have preferred to starve rather than go "on the town."

During spring, summer, and fall there was always plenty for these backwoods families to do to prepare for the long and rigorous winters. But when winter actually came, that was a vastly different matter. Outside of attending to the domestic animals and cutting the family supply of fuel, there was very little to occupy the time of the male members of the families. Being essentially pioneers, and possessing all the ambitious qualities necessary for wresting a living from a semi-wilderness, idle time hung heavily on their hands.

Accordingly, it was at this time of the year that "gumming" was most engaged in. Men and boys of the farming families followed the business from one end of the winter to the other. Trappers, after the snows became too deep for the successful pursuit of fur-bearers, took it up to round out the season's returns. And after the logs were all banked by the riversides in preparation for the breakup and the opening of the spring drives, lumberjacks occasionally followed the gum trails. A few made it a kind of profession, keeping at it throughout the year except for the very hottest months, at which times the gum would become soft and pitchy if removed from the trees.

When cleaned and ready for market, the gum was worth from eighty cents to a dollar a pound, according to the grade, and an experienced gummer could average about three pounds a day in good timber. Three dollars was considered excellent compensation for a day's work in those days of "trade wages."

Spruce gum is formed by the resin exuded by the tree for the purpose of sealing wounds and seams, and many of the shrewder pickers took advantage of the fact by cutting short gashes in the bark at the base of trees. These individuals had an eye for future business, for in the course of a year or so these wounds would yield large drips of pure, amber colored gum. However, this method was not greatly resorted to, as the owners of the timber lands frowned upon it. Anyway, there was always plenty of good picking timber available, and no very large territory could be thoroughly gone over in a day or a week. Trees that were partly dead usually proved to be the best yielders, and a man versed in the lore of gumming could spot one as far as he could see it. Some of these would yield a pound or more of gum.

Gum pickers usually traveled in pairs, but sometimes alone, and seldom more than three together. Their outfits were as light and compact as possible, as they carried them with them during the day and camped wherever night overtook them. A packbasket contained a few articles of staple foods such as salt pork or bacon, flour, salt, tea (coffee was a luxury in those days), a few potatoes, etc. Because few of them stayed more than three or four consecutive nights in the woods, they were able to carry small amount of baked goods also.

The culinary utensils consisted of a frying pan, a well-blackened tea pail, a couple of tin cups, and the same number of tin plates. The inevitable jack-knife carried by all woodsmen served as a means of conveying the food from the plate to the mouth, whenever the more simple expedient of using the fingers was not resorted to.

A light axe was strapped to the outside of the packbasket. Some few carried a gun on the chance of adding small game to the bill of fare, but this was seldom resorted to as a gun was considered just so much superfluous weight. Blankets were almost never carried, as these too were considered added weight even in the dead of winter.

When night came on, a camping place was selected and a fire built, usually against a giant hardwood or a huge, overturned root. A shelter consisting of a framework of poles with a heavy covering of evergreen branches was erected where the light and heat of the fire would be reflected into it, and the floor was covered a foot or so deep with more branches. Then, when the night's supply of wood had been dragged up, and the supper had been eaten, the gummers crawled into their little shanty, sometimes wet and cold, to smoke a pipe of Warnick-and-Brown tobacco, and spend the night as best they could. Oh, this gum-picking game was no racket for milk-sops and molly-coddles.

Of course, snowshoes were indispensable in this business, as the snow used to get real deep — six or seven feet in the gum country. Almost every type and design were used, but among the professionals the "bear-paw" models were greatly favored, as the rounded tails enabled the wearer to walk backwards around a tree as easily as forward. Practical men, were these gummers.

Outside of the other articles of outfit already named, each party of gummers also carried a "gum-pole," now almost as extinct as the dodo bird. This contrivance consisted of a can of heavy tin or light metal, firmly fixed to a long, slender pole. The can was usually about four inches in diameter and six to eight inches long, with the upper edge sharpened all the way around. This device was used in securing the drips of gum high above the ground, by placing the sharpened edge under the gum and prying upward, after which the displaced globule fell neatly into the can. The pole was often equipped with sliding points and could be extended to twenty feet or more, or telescoped for convenience in carrying.

When the men folks returned from a successful gumming trip, laden with twenty or thirty pounds of gum, then began the duties of the women, girls and small boys. Each separate chunk had to be carefully scraped to remove the murky outside sheen, after which the whole amount was divided into three distinct grades. The clear, amber drips composed the very choicest grade and commanded the highest prices. The duller, opaque pieces of a yellow or pink cast came next, and the "old gum," usually four or five years old, received third place and usually brought fifteen or twenty cents a pound. This latter grade was used for various commercial purposes, such as ingredients for paints and varnishes, while the better grades found their way into various medicines and ointments.

After the cleaning process was finished, the gum was then taken to market and sold. Usually any grocery or drug store had a ready outlet for all they could buy, and the gummer more often than not had to take his pay in "trade" from the store.

All this, of course, was long before the steadily increasing demand for lumber and paper-material brought about the destruction of the great spruce forests. It is very doubtful if there is a place left in New York State where three pounds of spruce gum could be found in a day. In fact, it is almost impossible in most localities to find enough for a good chew. Be that as it may, gum-picking as a business has vanished from sight, gone the way of the buffalo and the passenger pigeon.

DINNER BY
THE POUND

During the many years since they were first settled, the twin villages of Sandy Creek and Lacona, which once was designated as Sandy Creek Station, have known many famous eating places.

The historic old Thomas House (now Hotel Martin) in Sandy Creek at one time enjoyed wide-spread fame for its bountiful chicken and steak dinners; and in Lacona the Plummer Hotel and the Union Center House were only slightly less noted for their fine foods and hospitality. Also located in this village was a place known as Kelsey's Restaurant, outstanding because of its succulent oyster stew and fish dinners, in which it specialized.

This establishment was owned and run by one Elisha Kelsey, better known as plain Lish (with a long i); a large, robust, and very jolly man. Lish always allowed that he wanted to be buried in a hemlock coffin, "So I can go through Hell a-crackin," he used to say. While he perhaps did not realize the very letter of his wish, he came reasonably close to it in one respect and is now buried beneath a finely sculptured replica of a hemlock stump.

Most of the teamsters who used to draw lumber, logs, and tan-bark from Boyston and Redfield for a living, patronized Kelsey's place for the mid-day meal. Here they always received a good feed for their money, and the fun-loving proprietor always made them feel welcome, no matter how patched or horsey-smelling their clothing might be.

One man who hailed from up around Diamond, in the town of Worth, was a pretty steady customer at Lish's place. This man was large and brawny, and had an appetite to go with his size. Lish used to joke with him about his eating capabilities, telling him that the restaurant lost money every time he came in, and that he guessed they'd better start charging him for his dinners by the pound, rather than by the meal.

The customer accepted this levity with good nature, and one day when Lish made this suggestion he countered with a proposition of his own.

"Tell you what I'll do," he said. "The next time I come in I *will* pay by the pound. You can weigh me when I come in, and weigh me again when I leave, and I'll pay you eight shillin' (ninety-six cents, by their system of reckoning) for every pound I've gained."

Lish was quick to jump at the offer not seeing how it was possible for him to lose.

"But there's one condition," went on the man. "If I *lose* weight while I'm in here, you pay me the same for every pound I lose."

Still not seeing how it was possible for him to come out on the small end of the deal, Lish stuck to his agreement and the two men shook hands on the proposition.

A few days later the Diamond man again appeared at the restaurant, and as it was a cold day he was wearing a long overcoat. Lish was ready for him, and marched him into a nearby hardware store where his weight was taken and duly recorded before witnesses. He jokingly warned the man that he'd better be wearing the coat again at weigh-out time, just in case he had the pockets loaded with lead, and to this the customer laughingly agreed. What Lish did not know was that beneath the coat the fellow had wrapped a ten-pound log chain around his waist.

Well, they went into the restaurant and the meal began. Lish really piled the food on the customer's plate and watched it disappear with a great deal of satisfaction, chuckling to himself as he mentally calculated what the meal was going to cost the man.

The eater did not seem to be the least bit worried in this respect, and went on devouring the food with a regular logging-camp appetite. At first he kept his long coat on, but as soon as he had a chance to shed the log chain and hide it under the table, he did so and laid the garment aside.

After having consumed enough food for three normal men, he at last pushed back his chair and announced that he guessed maybe he'd had enough.

"Now don't get away from the table hungry," urged Lish. "Sure you can't eat any more?" After all, eight shillings a pound was a right good price for food.

The man allowed that he couldn't eat another bite, and Lish grinned.

"Good," he said. "Come on . . . it's time to settle up."

The customer put on his overcoat and followed Lish back into the hardware store, where several men were waiting to learn the outcome of the affair. One can well imagine the restaurant owner's look of disbelief when the scales announced the man's weight to now be about five pounds less than it had been before.

Knowing full well that he had been hoaxed in some manner, Lish weighed the man a couple of times more, but still the tally remained the same.

"Looks like you owe me about forty shillin'," grinned the man from Diamond.

Crestfallen and very mystified, Lish joined rather feebly into the laughter at his expense, paid the man the money, and returned to his restaurant. It was not until he was cleaning up the place that evening that he found the chain and understood how the hoax had been worked.

A few days later the Diamond man stopped in to pay back the forty shillings, and the two enjoyed a big laugh over the incident.

"Well, I had the best of the deal anyway," remarked the restaurant owner. "Your chain was worth all of that."

" 'Twan't mine to begin with," grinned the man. "I got it out of your horse-barn just afore I come in."

THE MISMATCHED MICHIGANDER

Back in the roistering old days three-quarters of a century ago, one of the more gentle past-times prevalent in bar-rooms and lumber camp lobbies was known as shin-kicking. This was at one time on a popularity par with Indian wrestling and wrist-twisting among the rough-and-ready element who made their precarious living on timber drives and in the lumbering woods. Its practice died out quicker because of the serious consequences often attendant upon such contests.

To play at this game, two men, usually about matched as to height and weight, would stand facing one another, each with his hands upon the other's shoulders. At a given signal, each would balance upon one leg, the matter of whether left or right having been decided upon beforehand. With his free foot, each would then proceed to belabor his opponent's stationary underpinning with all the speed, power, and ferocity possible. The first contestant to remove his hands and retreat, or in any other manner indicate that he had taken sufficient punishment, lost the contest and his opponent was declared the winner.

The rules of the game were very few. The challenged man had the right to choose the leg upon which he wished to stand, and the challenger had to go along with his choice. Sharp calks in the shoes were prohibited, but hob-nails were not. Usually the contests were short and sharp, no one caring to stand the pain for very long. Sometimes a contestant's leg was actually broken, but this did not happen often. Usually the direct outcome was a sore and swollen shin for a few days.

As in any other sport, some men came to excel in shin-kicking, and kicked their way up to become local champions. These were occasionally matched against one another, and the betting on these occasions was often fast and furious.

Being short and stocky of build, and possessing the inborn traits of grit and tenacity natural to his Dutch ancestry, John Bush soon became known and recognized as one of these champions. This was in the days when as a young man he followed the lumber-woods calling; years before he retired to become a farmer in Boylston, and gain fame as a bear- and bee-hunter.

One time Bush was working in a large lumber camp up near Hooker, in Lewis County. In that camp, as in many others, he soon was recognized as the champion shin-kicker, by virtue of having taken on and defeated all challengers to his title.

One day the camp-boss returned from a trip to Lowville, bringing with him a new man whom he said he had hired as a teamster. This seemed rather strange to the few who bothered to give it any thought, as the camp already had enough teamsters on hand.

This stranger, who announced that he was a native of the Michigan forests, was a rather nondescript appearing sort of fellow. His right arm was shorter than the left, one eye was grey and the other blue, and he walked with a limp. As one old-timer put it, "He was kind of mismatched all around."

The first day that he was in camp, the boss casually

92

let drop the information that he was a shin-kicker of no mean ability. By night this news had traveled the grape-vine route and gotten to Bush, who right away decided that there would have to be a showdown. It was unthinkable that there should be two good shin-kickers in the same camp without a contest to decide who was top man, and the sooner this came about the better.

Accordingly, that very evening when the men had finished their supper and were gathered in the lobby to smoke and swap yarns until bed-time, Bush approached the stranger and engaged him in conversation. He wasted very little time on preliminaries, but came quickly to the point.

"Hear you was quite a shin-kicker back in Michigan," he remarked.

"Why, yes, I've kicked some," admitted the man modestly, squinting his blue eye.

"Well, I'm knowed as the bull shin-kicker around here," said Bush a little truculently. "D' you want to try me out?"

"Don't know as I do," asserted the stranger, squinting his grey eye.

"Well, I wanta try you out," said Bush, knocking the ashes from his pipe. "So mister, you'd better git ready to kick."

"S'pose I gotta oblige you," said the man from Michigan, standing up.

The conversation among the other men in the lobby had suddenly died out, as their attention became riveted upon the exchange between these two. This development had been anticipated, and already speculation as to the outcome of the imminent encounter was rife.

Popular opinion was naturally in favor of the camp champion, but this was not so unanimous that long-odds money against the underdog was not readily accepted. As the two men made their preparation for the contest, bets were offered and taken; and a careful observer would have noticed that the camp boss placed a goodly amount of money, at one against two, on the man from Michigan.

"Which leg?" asked Bush, the challenger, as the two antagonists faced each other and placed hands on shoulders. By this he of course indicated that the other man had the choice of which leg he wished to stand on.

"Left," said the Michigander, and each poised on his left leg.

At the signal to begin, Bush launched a savage kick at his opponent's shin, and the toe of his heavy brogan met the target squarely and with a solid whack. But so far as could be judged by the man's facial expression, he did not appear to have even felt the blow.

At the same time, his right toe met Bush's left shin with an impact that sent slivers of pain shooting up the latter's leg. But Bush only gritted his teeth and settled grimly down to business. This wasn't going to be so danged easy as he had anticipated.

For the next couple of minutes the punishment was fast and furious. Bush's attack was swift and ferocious, and a little desperate. Here he was doing his dangdest, and each kick was jarring the Michigan man clear to his shoulders, yet he displayed no outward sign of distress or even discomfort. What kind of man was this, he wondered.

On the other hand, the Michigander's steady and measured pace was beginning to tell. Bush's leg was fast becoming a mass of throbbing pain, which threatened to double up at any minute and send him crashing down to defeat. But his Dutch obstinacy caused him to hang on, and he launched a last desperate effort; which like the others seemed to have absolutely no effect.

At last the inevitable happened. Bush's tortured leg refused to support his weight any longer, and he rolled to the floor, his face twisted with pain. Calmly, the Michigander reached down, grasped him by the arm, and hoisted him to his feet.

"Reckon you're satisfied now," was all he said as the jubilant lumberjacks who had backed him in the betting flocked around to congratulate him.

Bush was a good loser, but as he doused his sore and bleeding shin with turpentine and horse-linament, a suspicion that he had somehow been duped was already taking hold in his mind, and he voiced his intention of challenging the new champion to a return match as soon as possible.

But as it turned out, this was never to take place. When the camp awoke the next morning, the man from Michigan has disappeared, lock, stock, and barrel. With him had gone a goodly bite of the betting money, and none of them ever saw him again.

While the camp boss must have known that a hoax had been perpetrated, he kept his own council. It was not until a few weeks later, during a trip into Lowville, that Bush learned the secret of the Michigan man's amazing stamina, which was somewhat in accord with what he had suspected all along. Some years before, the fellow's left leg had been amputated at the knee, following an accident in a sawmill, and the one on which he now limped around was made out of wood.

In later years, Bush derived a great deal of enjoyment out of relating the story of his encounter with the "mismatched Michigander."

RESURRECTION, AND
NOT MANY THERE

A few miles north of the uppermost tip of Tug Hill, where the Indian River makes a gigantic loop before straightening out upon its northward sweep toward Black Lake, stands the picturesque village of Theresa.

First visited in 1810 by M. James LeRay de Chaumont, who owned vast tracts of land in what are now Jefferson and Lewis counties, the locality was instantly recognized as an ideal spot for a village. At this point the river rushed over a sheer ledge of rock fifty-five feet in height, furnishing limitless water power for the many mills and factories that M. LeRay envisioned there .

With this thought in mind, he immediately commissioned Muscrove Evans to survey a lot one thousand acres in extent, surrounding the site on all sides. This he set aside as a reservation to later be divided into village lots, designating at the time that all lots to be used for churches or schools should be furnished free of charge, except for the cost of the deeds. He then named the community Theresa, in honor of his only daughter.

The river derived its name from the many members of the Iroquois tribes who each year came there to hunt and trap. For twenty miles below the high falls the stream was winding and leisurely, running through low, marshy areas that were favorite breeding places for mink, muskrats, otter, and beaver. The surrounding forests were plentifully supplied with deer, bear, panther,

97

wolves, and smaller game and fur-bearers; and the streams were alive with trout and other fish. Small wonder, then, that the territory was so popular with the dusky hunters . . . or that they so disliked to give it up.

For the first few years Theresa grew somewhat slowly, but in 1819 M. LeRay had a sawmill and gristmill built, thinking that this would stimulate the sale of his lands. This proved to be true, and from that time on the growth of the village was much more rapid. The first school was erected in 1821, and for some years was also used for holding church services.

Industry began to settle there, lured by the cheap and abundant waterpower, and from then on the settlement grew by leaps and bounds. By 1855 the place contained the following enterprises: Two gristmills with nine run of stone; three sawmills; two foundries; two machine shops; one woolen mill with three hundred spindles; one plaster mill; three lath and shingle mills; two carriage shops; two cabinet shops; one chair factory; six shoe shops; one marble shop; one tannery; four blacksmith shops; two tailor shops; two harness shops; one goldsmith; one fishing tackle manufactory; two taverns; four dry-goods stores; four grocerys; and two pot and pearl asheries. At this time over two hundred craftsmen of various kinds were employed by these establishments.

In 1859 and 1890, the village was visited by two disastrous fires, from the last of which it never fully recovered. Today it is a still beautiful but somewhat somnolent little community, basking in the reflected glory of a past that at one time threatened to make it the metropolis of the North Country.

It was sometime during this golden age that there occurred an incident which has caused a great deal of merriment in the retelling. It concerned one W. A.

Fisher, the local undertaker, and an experience that befell him.

It seems that Mr. Fisher had an out-of-town funeral scheduled for the next day, with the burial to be in a somewhat distant cemetery. As this was in the days of slow horse-and-wagon travel, and the funeral was to be rather early, he accordingly made all possible preparations the night before. Most of his equipment was stored in the hearse, with the exception of the rough-box, which was too heavy to load without help. This was placed beside the board-walk in front of his establishment, ready to be loaded bright and early in the morning.

Now the village, like most small towns, possessed a "character;" in this case a ne'er-do-well Irishman by the very Hibernian name of Clancy, well liked for his good nature and ready wit. Along about midnight, Clancy came weaving up the main street after an evening of conviviality in a local tavern, carrying quite a cargo of alcoholic cheer and making rather heavy going of it. Somewhere near the undertaking parlor the cargo got the better of him and he folded up on the grass beside the walk.

Some time later several young men were passing by and noticed Clancy, stretched out on his back and snoring peacefully. After a short consultation they decided that he shouldn't be left lying there to catch pneumonia. Casting about for a safe place to put him, someone noticed the rough-box standing beside the sidewalk, and removing the cover, they lifted him and placed him gently inside. The cover was then put back lightly, so as not to deprive him of air, after which his benefactors stole softly away.

At just about the crack of dawn the next morning, Mr. Fisher came hurrying down to his place of business, noting with pleasure that it was going to be a good day.

As he passed the rough-box he gave it a resounding thump with his fist. A moment later, as he was unlocking the door, he thought he heard a sound; and turning his head he saw with amazement that the cover of the box was moving.

The next moment the cover slid back and Clancy sat up abruptly, a look of stupefied surprise on his face.

"Why hello, Mr. Fisher," he greeted the astonished undertaker. "It is Mr. Fisher, is it not?"

"Yes, it's me alright," Mr. Fisher assured him, "But what in tarnation are you doing in there, anyway?"

The Irishman's eyes turned reverently to the east, where a flaring sunrise was just beginning to paint the skies, and slowly a big grin spread over his face.

"Hiven be praised," he exclaimed joyfully. "Here 'tis a grand and glorious Resurrection Morn, and only the two of us turned up to answer the call."

HIGH JINKS ON
THE STATE MEADOWS

Many years ago, there used to exist on the upper reaches of Mad River, in the town of Montague, what was then known as the State Beaver Meadows.

This area was composed of a series of meadow-like openings situated along both banks of the river, and connected to one another in such a way as to form a clearing containing many acres of extremely fertile land. It was first formed many years before by a succession of gigantic beaver ponds which, the dams that had caused their being having fallen into disrepair, had gradually drained themselves. The river had dropped back into its original bed, leaving the surrounding area covered by a deep, rich bed of silt and topsoil.

For many, many years, until the clearing eventually grew back up to alders and brush, this ground annually grew a large crop of succulent wild hay known as bluejoint. The grass often grew head-high, and was highly valued as horse fodder by the numerous lumbering concerns in the area. The meadows were state-owned and the crop thus became the property of anyone who harvested it, which the lumber companies usually did.

As the ground in the meadows was soft and spongy, the hay could not be harvested by horse-power, This made it necessary to cut, rake, and stack the crop by hand; the stacks being built on pole racks to protect them from high water. When winter came and the soft soil froze hard, the hay could then be transported by teams and sleighs.

All this hand harvesting made it necessary for the lumber companies to hire many men and boys to do the mowing with hand-scythes. Large numbers of the male population for miles around used to hire out during haying, living in the camps maintained by the various lumber concerns for the purpose. The work was hard, but the pay and the eats were generally good, and some of the best hand-mowers in the country used to congregate there.

Naturally, considerable rivalry existed among these gentlemen of the hand-scythe. Numerous contests were arranged and carried out, accenting such mowing skills as width and straightness of swath, cleanness of cut, and speed in covering a certain distance.

One of the most popular contests was a race between two teams of from four to six mowers each. In this test a certain area of meadow, usually an acre in extent, was paced off and divided equally down the middle. Each team then mowed a half, and the group which finished its section first won the contest. To make the game more interesting, each contestant was required to put up an entrance fee, all the fees going into a jackpot which was split up by the winning side. Many side bets were also placed, both by contestants and the onlookers. It was during one of these contests that there occurred an incident which has afforded much merriment in the retelling.

One summer in the '90's the Hooker Lumber Company and the Longstrife Lumber Company maintained adjacent hay camps on the meadows. Both had crack teams of scythemen, and a good deal of bickering existed between the two groups. As was almost inevitable, someone suggested a race, and a challenge was given and accepted. The entrance fee was fixed high enough to make the affair really interesting, and the time of the contest was fixed for the following Sunday, rain or shine.

All week long the interest in the coming event continued to mount apace. Bets were offered and covered, and the excitement swiftly grew. The Longstrife outfit was generally conceded to have a slight edge, but the Hooker combine was very determined to win, and anything might happen.

The day of the contest came at last, and a beautiful morning it turned out to be, with a promise of hot weather later on. Accordingly, it was decided to hold the match soon after breakfast, while it was still fairly cool, and a square acre was staked out and divided down the middle. Straws were drawn to determine which team mowed on which side. Scythes which had been carefully ground and whetted half the night before were brought out and adjusted. At sharp eight o'clock the word was given, and the blue-joint began to fall.

Now it was the custom during these affairs for each team to have a jug of hard cider, which had been cooling all night in a deep hole in the river, at one end of the field. From this each member took a big swig upon the completion of a turn around the course. This served the double purpose of quenching the thirst and acting as a spur to greater efforts, and often proved an important factor in the outcome of a contest. So it was to prove in this instance, but in a vastly different way than was anticipated by most.

Scarcely two laps had been completed when the Longstrife team began to fulfill expectations by moving ahead of their opponents, and by the time the jug had yielded up its third round they were half a lap ahead.

It was right after they had turned and started back down the course that something occurred which was witnessed by only a couple of people.

A long, hooked stick snaked swiftly out of the tall grass near the jug, hooked into its handle, and it was drawn quickly back out of sight. Almost at once another jug, identical in shape and size, was thrust back out to take its place.

This vessel also contained hard cider just as cool and refreshing as the other, but with one very great difference. Into it had been introduced a goodly amount of jallop, a sweet-tasting substance well known in those days for its quick, complete, and unfailing catharctic propensities.

As the race progressed the pace grew faster and faster. Soon the Hooker team was a full lap behind, with the Longstrife combine appearing stronger by the minute. Then, at about the eighth lap, things really began to happen.

One of the leading men in the Longstrife team suddenly threw down his scythe and made a rush for a clump of alders at the end of the course. Hardly had he reached his destination when another team-mate did the same, heading in another direction but in no less of a hurry.

Inside of five minutes the entire Longstrife team were forced to answer urgent and mysterious calls of nature, accompanied by the jeers and wise-cracks of their opponents. One man failed to make it quite in time, and forthwith became a sort of social outcast for the rest of the match. At one time it might even have been assumed that their activities were responsible for the old cliche: "Two comin' . . . two goin' . . . two busy . . . and two mowin'."

Of course all this activity lost them a great deal of ground, and by the time they had settled back to the business in hand, the Hooker group was half a lap ahead. And they had not succeeded in gaining back very much distance when the second series of visitations overtook them and the whole thing happened over again.

This proved to be the final catastrophy, and they lost so much ground that they never had a chance after that. The Hooker boys were a shoo-in for an easy victory, wrestling from their rivals the coveted title of King Mowers of the State Meadows.

Be it everlastingly to their credit that they had no part in the conspiracy which led to their somewhat tarnished victory. One of the spectators had conceived and carried out the entire plot in order to win a two-dollar bet.

THE HUNGRY NINE

Along during the first two decades of the present century, the people of the nation became increasingly sports minded. Hitherto, boxing and wrestling had been about the only sports that were enthusiastically followed, with only a minimum of interest being shown in games requiring team-play. But suddenly baseball zoomed into national prominence, and the change made itself felt in the rural areas as well as in the cities.

In the Tug Hill regions every little community organized its own team which it supported loyally; for, as the saying goes, "fun, money, or marbles." These teams were composed almost entirely of young farmers and lumberjacks, and were generally poorly equipped. Those who could not afford baseball gloves utilized other types of handgear, or played bare-handed, protected only by the hard callouses produced by steady contact with axe-halves or plow-handles. Bats were usually home made affairs, carefully hewed, shaved, and sanded from hickory or white ash to suit the individual users' personal tastes. Playing diamonds were laid out in someone's meadow that was fairly free from hollows and cradle-knolls.

Usually each team possessed but one baseball. Home-runs were few and far between. If the ball went over the fence into someone's pasture or woodlot, a limit of two bases was an established rule, while the ball was hunted up and returned to the playing field. In at least one incident that caused a great deal of amusement, time out was

107

called while the ball was retrieved from a recently deposited cow-flop in which it nestled, after which it was gingerly wiped off and tossed back into the game.

Uniforms were exceedingly un-uniform. Oftentimes matching caps were the only means of distinguishing one team from the other. Frequently this was the only departure from everyday attire. Footwear might range from cowhide boots to canvas "sneaks." Often a game was played in calked "Croghan" shoes, a type of heavy and durable footwear much favored by pulp peelers and river-drivers.

What these "town teams" lacked in present-day polish and finesse they more than made up for in drive and enthusiasm. Competitive spirit ran high and sometimes unchecked, often developing into pugilistic affairs that sent more than one player home with a black eye or bloody nose. The position of umpire was an unenviable one, and was usually filled by an individual large and tough enough to enforce his decisions against all comers.

These organizations bore a variety of catchy and descriptive names, such as Woodchucks, Bearcats, and Flying Squirrels. Redfield had its Red Foxes; the Blount Lumber Company their Hardwood Slivers. Probably one of the most picturesquely named, as well as being one of the best from a games-won standpoint, was Boylston's "Hungry Nine."

The manner in which this team won its comical moniker involves an amusing incident that demands retelling. It all came about on one Fourth of July on which Boylston was playing Redfield, another exceedingly strong team, on the latter's home field. As usual, the game was fast, furious, and well contested, but due to a series of unfortunate occurrences, the Red Foxes were the losers. Sixty or more years have erased from memory the actual score, but history has it that it was exceedingly lop-sided and aroused the ire of the folks of Redfield to a fever pitch.

This is not so strange when one considers how loyally these town teams were supported by their respective communities. To live in a particular place was to back the home team lock, stock, and barrel.

Certainly the people of Redfield could never be accused of being poor sports, and maybe the Boylston boys bragged just a little. Anyway, the displeasure of the folks in the village began to make itself evident in an unusual manner.

Soon after the game was over the appetites of the victorious Boyston team began to make themselves felt. Accordingly, they trooped into one of the town's two hotels to appease their hunger, only to be accosted by the landlord.

"Sorry boys," he said. "I'm full up. Can't feed another soul. You'll have to go somewhere else."

Argument produced no results except to strengthen the hotel owner's determination, so the hungry group made their way to the other hotel. Here the result was the same, no food.

"Just run out of grub, boys," alibied this owner. "Won't have no more today. You'll hafta go some'ers else." This in spite of the fact that the now really hungry team could look directly into the dining room where many local people were leisurely eating.

Somewhat desperate now, and with the pangs of hunger momentarily becoming more acute, the victorious group, with taste of victory now decidedly sour, decided to visit a grocery store to purchase crackers, cheese, and whatever else was available for a makeshift meal. But here their luck was no better. The storekeeper flatly refused to sell them as much as a crumb, and this was the prevailing theme. No store or individual would sell or give them a bite to eat.

By the time they had exhausted the last possibility of being fed, their hunger had reached gargantuan proportions. Ahead of them was a ten mile trip home, which must be made on foot or with a couple of one-horse rigs which they had. With extremely low spirit and very lean bellies they set out. At the first farmhouse that they came to they stopped and tried to buy food, but they were politely and firmly refused. This happened again and again, until they had reached a point some miles away.

Finally they just gave up and slogged doggedly on toward home, which they reached long after dark, victorious and famished.

It is a known fact that all members survived the ordeal of starvation to which they had been subjected. But as news of the amusing incident spread, they were promptly and appropriately dubbed "The Hungry Nine," a name that was borne proudly by themselves and their successors through several playing seasons, until their final dissolution.

Note: The last remaining member of the original "Hungry Nine," Mr. Earl Noble, died June 5, 1970, at the ripe old age of nearly eighty years. Mr. Noble was a successful lumberman all his life except for a few years during World War II, when he served as a government lumber inspector and consultant. Later, he moved to the village of Redfield, where he served as Town Supervisor for several years. He was an ardent harness racing fan and horse owner, and died very suddenly at Vernon Downs after watching one of his horses win first place.

JAY BARNES

Nearly everyone who lived in the territory between Tug Hill and Lake Ontario during the couple of decades on either side of the turn of the century, was familiar with a character named Jay Barnes. Housewives, farmers, lumberjacks, school children ... veritably the whole rural population knew, liked, and respected him; and welcomed him whenever he came around.

Mr. Barnes was a very large, very corpulent, and very florid gentleman, who roved the countryside from early spring until late fall, perched atop the high, swaying seat of a jangling tin-cart. From this lofty throne he transacted as much of his business as possible, due to the fact that the rotundity of his form made it rather hard for him to mount and dismount.

Many days, it was said, he carried on a full day's business with only one trip down to terra firma; that being at whichever farmhouse he stopped for the noon meal. Much of his stock he could reach with a long wire hook which he carried for the purpose; for the rest the customer had to depend to a large degree upon his own efforts at selection. It might be said that Jay was one of the first exponents of the serve-yourself policy which has since become so universal.

However, sometimes the article desired might be buried deep within the jangling clutter that filled the inside of the cart, safe from discovery by even the most patient customer. At such times, Mr. Barnes used his not un-

111

talented powers of persuasion in an effort to convince the customer that what he or she really wanted was some other, and more readily accessible, substitute. This attempt failing, he would roll from the high wagon-seat, seemingly headed for certain destruction by spattering on the hard ground, but always recovering himself just in the nick of time and landing on his feet as nimbly as a cat.

Locomotion for the tin emporium was furnished over the years by a succession of disreputable looking horses, selected for their muscularity and amiability rather than for their fine appearance. Chief among these was Old Nob, a big-jointed, sway-backed, dapple-gray who had managed to absorb a portion of his master's devil take-it attitude, and so served faithfully, if somewhat lackadaisically, for several years. Old Nob never traveled faster than a walk, and always fell asleep promptly the moment he heard the word "whoa." Some said that he also enjoyed an occasional nap while under motion. This supposition seemed to be somewhat proven by the fact that once, while his master was also stealing a few winks, he walked smack into the tail-end of a load of lumber stuck fast in a mud-hole.

Mr. Barnes carried on his wagon a large, gaily-striped umbrella bearing an advertisement for Somebody-or-Other's Colic Cure. When set into a ring fastened to the wagon seat, it alternately furnished shelter against sudden shower and summer heat. He also carried a long, rawhide-lashed whip with which he occasionally tickled the back-side of any stray dog presumptious enough to leap at either the horse or wagon.

Not the least of his accomplishments was a deadly accuracy with a stream of tobacco juice, as many a blue-bottle and unwary butterfly found out to their sorrow.

112

Anyone whom Jay encountered along the roads or in the adjacent fields . . . man, woman, or child . . . was a potential source of gossip and information, and never did he fail to stop and pass the time of day. Sometimes these little chats extended to an hour or over; but of course a few minutes lost here and there meant not nearly so much as they do in this hurry-up age. Neighborliness was of paramount importance, and on this commodity Jay stinted not in the slightest.

But sometimes it was quite some distance between houses and between conversations, and in these solitary interludes Jay entertained himself by either conversing with Old Nob, or singing the tunes popular in those times, in a rather high whiskey-tenor which carried a considerable distance on a clear day.

Many a small country boy, busy with gathering the eggs or splitting the evening kindling wood, had suddenly straightened up to listen; and hearing the sound of slightly off-key singing accompanied by the jingle of the tin-cart, had run into the house shouting, "Ma, Jay's comin. I kin hear him singin. Kin we have him stay all night, Ma? Kin we?"

Lucky indeed did the family with whom Mr. Barnes spent the night consider itself. He brought news of the outside world at a time when news, in the rural regions, was at a premium. And more important, he brought entertainment. His sense of humor was known far and wide, and his stock of amusing anecdotes and personal experiences was well nigh inexhaustable.

Many an evening did he sit regaling an appreciative audience with happenings real and fancied until long after honest, hard-working folks should have been in bed. Often youths and oldsters alike would walk long distances to spend the evening with a family where the tin-cart put up for the night.

Very few families ever wanted to accept pay for his board and lodging, but he always insisted on paying, with articles from his stock of merchandise. Being so exceedingly corpulent, it was very hard for him to bend over to tie his shoes, so he usually figured to "hire" some small boy or girl to do it for him.

Most of the time he was neat and clean, but he had one very unsanitary habit that probably won him more disfavor with neat housewives than any other thing he ever did. This was the custom of drying out his used quids of chewing tobacco on the hearth of the kitchen stove, later to be tucked away in a little cloth bag in readiness for smoking in his rank old corncob pipe.

As I have said, his sharp and rather dry sense of humor was well known, and many amusing tales are told concerning his sayings and doings. Some of these have probably gained considerably in scope and coloring by repeated retelling, but some still bear the brand of authenticity, judging by known habits and characteristics of the subject. One of these latter concerns an erstwhile canine companion of Mr. Barnes.

It seems that this long-eared old black-and-tan hound adopted Jay and his outfit early one spring, and traveled with him one complete season, foraging as he went. Old Sport, as he came to be known, was a wide ranger and sometimes worked far to one side or ahead of the tin-cart.

One day when Jay was on the road between Lacona and Smartville, the old hound, ranging far ahead as usual, came upon and devoured a freshly baked pie that had been set outside by a housewife to cool. When Jay

114

drove up a few minutes later, it was to be confronted by a very irate lady indeed.

"Jay Barnes, you owe me twenty-five cents," she shouted almost as soon as he hove into sight.

Jay sat bolt upright on his seat. "Whoa," he said to the horse.

"Why hello there, Allie," he said to the lady. "What's that you say about me owin' you two shilling?"

"That's what I said, alright," said the housewife vociferously. "Two shillin' for the pie that danged dog of yourn just et up. Had it coolin' right there on that bench an' he came along an' gobbled it."

"Well now, Allie, that's sure too bad," said Jay soothingly. "What kind of a pie was it anyway?"

"It was an apple pie, that's what kind it was," returned the lady irritably. "Why? What difference does it make?"

"Makes lots of difference," grinned Jay. "You see, I know now it must have been some other dog that et your pie. Couldn't have been mine, because he never eats apple pie without cheese, an' I ain't heard you mention any cheese. Good day, Allie. Giddap Nob."

And he drove away leaving a very red-faced but amused lady behind.

Another tale points out the fact that Mr. Barnes was an occasional pal of John Barleycorn. While never an excessive drinker, like most men of his time, he did at times imbibe more than was strictly good for him.

On one of these occasions he decided to make an unscheduled descent from the wagon after stopping in the dooryard of a customer. Rolling from the high seat in the usual manner, he somehow forgot the last feat of gymnastics necessary to land him on his feet. Instead, he hit the hard frozen ground with a tremendous crash, accompanied by several articles of his noisy merchandise.

Bouncing to a sitting position, he let out an angry roar.

"Who the hell put that extra step in there?" he bellowed.

"Did you hurt yourself, Mr. Barnes?" asked the excited housewife as she dashed out the door. By this time his habitual jocularity was beginning to return.

"Hell no, Sarry," he grinned sheepishly, as he clambered painfully to his feet. "Didn't you know? . . . I always get off that way?"

Jay owned a small farm at the foot of the Wheat Hill, a couple of miles out east of Lacona, and here he made his headquarters between trips on the road and during off seasons.

It is said that one time he promised to pay the bill of a local doctor with a load of hay, to be delivered to the physician's barn in Lacona. Time ran on and on, and no hay arrived; until one day Jay met the doctor's rig on the Ridge Road, down toward Richland. True to form, they stopped to visit for a while.

"Say, Jay," commented the medic a little sarcastically, "That certainly was a dandy load of hay that you brought me."

"Well now, Doc, I'm sure glad you liked it," said Jay. "I feel the same way about your doctorin'. Tell you what I'm goin' to do. I'm gonna bring you another load out of the same mow, and it won't cost you a cent."

Typical sprinkler used to keep hauling roads frozen.

Loading logs at skidway. (Photo by Dewitt Wiley)

Hauling logs with Linns on Elmer Bernier's Tug Hill job.

River driver, using a peavey, breaking up a log wing. (U.S. Forest Service photo)

*Three Caster brothers. From left:
Clyde, Billie Ward, and Beartrap.*

*"Billie Ward" Caster, a professor of
woodsology.*

*The trap that "Beartrap" Caster set
bare-handed.*

Oswelewgois (Oswego-Lewis) Club near Redfield, 1911.

Earl Noble in his ball playing days. Mr. Noble was the longest surviving member of the original "Hungry Nine," famous old sandlot team.

"Hardwood" Jones, working in open blacksmith shop. Hardwood is on left.

The horse furnished the power on log
skidding and hauling for most of a
century. (Fynmore photo)

Horses on George Colvin's Tug Hill logging operations. *(Fynmore photo)*

George Colvin, camp operator, and Ernie Hebert, camp foreman, plan logging job. *(Fynmore photo)*

The cook in a logging camp prepares for the evening meal. (Fynmore photo)

Lumberjacks at lunch in the cook camp. (Fynmore photo)

THE DEATH OF
A KILLER

Black bears can at times be termed cute and even comical, in fact they are recognized as being the clowns of the whole bear family because of their amusing traits and antics. But sometimes they were a headache and a real menace to the old-time pioneer settler in backwoods communities.

In the old days every farmer, large or small, kept a flock of sheep. These animals were raised both for their fleece and the meat which they produced, and were a very important factor in the economy of the times.

Now bears also had a taste for mutton, and felt no qualms whatever about going into a farmer's flock and helping themselves. While not all bears were sheep-killers, very few that had an opportunity to sample the meat were ever again satisfied with conventional Bruin fare, and in many cases became inveterate killers. These individuals inflicted great havoc among the wooly flocks, sometimes charging in among their terrified victims and killing as many as possible without rhyme or reason; eating only a small portion of each, or in some instances none at all.

Needless to say, the farmers who were victims of these forays rose in righteous wrath against the transgressors, and organized hunts to track them down and exterminate them. Often these hunts were successful, and the occasion of one of the predators being brought down caused great excitement and rejoicing. One such happening even caused a local newspaper to print a special supplement describing the event.

This sheet was issued by *The Sandy Creek News* and bears the date line of May 12, 1877. Across its face in flaring black headlines appear the following words:

KILLED
A Big Black Bear
In Boylston
Weight 370 pounds.

HE DIES "GAME"
After a Long Chase

The Dead Bear on Exhibition in
TOWN!
Now Sheep Can "Have a Rest"

The writer has had the pleasure of examining this account, but since it is somewhat given to flamboyant phrasing rather than attention to detail, he prefers to tell the story in his own words. In this he was given invaluable aid by Thomas W. Hamer, who is a son of the principal character concerned. While this event took place the year of Mr. Hamer's birth, he remembers having heard it discussed many times by his parents and their neighbors.

For some time the neighborhood had been bothered by numerous attacks on its flocks, apparently all by the same animal, which had proved too cunning to ever allow a hunter to get within shooting distance. During the previous fall 23 sheep had been killed, and so far that spring 32 more had been wantonly slaughtered.

118

One morning in early May, a farmer by the name of David Huffstater, who lived on the Smartville Road near what was known as the Second Gulf, discovered the mangled bodies of four of his animals in the bottom of the gulf not far from his home. Only small portions of the carcasses had been eaten, and all signs pointed to the havoc having been wrought by the same killer that had been pestering the neighborhood.

Mounting a horse, he hurried to the home of Thomas Hamer, Sr., who ran a large farm nearby and was known to be a very skillful hunter. Upon hearing the news Mr. Hamer immediately accompanied Huffstater back to the scene of the outrage, where they proceeded to look the situation over.

The men believed that the killer might return to its prey when prompted by hunger, and on this hope they based their plan of action. They knew it would be useless to lie in ambush, as this had been tried before without success; but they did believe that a cleverly concealed set-gun might do the trick.

Accordingly, they placed four muskets, which had been heavily charged with powder and buckshot, in positions where one gun covered each of the slain sheep, at about the height of a normal bear's body from the ground. To the trigger of each gun was fastened a thin, strong cord, the other end of which was attached to the bait in such a way that the slightest tug would discharge the weapon.

Two or three nights went by and nothing happened, and the hunter's hopes of success had begun to wane. Then one night about 9:30 Huffstater was awakened by the discharge of one of the set-guns. Leaping upon his horse he galloped to the Hamer home, where Mr. Hamer hastily armed himself and they returned to the scene, ac-

119

companied by a young fellow named Alfred Schermerhorn.

Immediately upon their arrival at the trap they discovered a heavy trail of blood leading away up the gulf. In spite of the fact that a wounded bear can be a very dangerous customer even in broad daylight, the three men immediately took up the chase, armed only with one gun (a .38 caliber double-barrelled rifle) and a lantern that shed only a desultory light.

The blood-trail led north, passing through a stone culvert beneath the Lacona-Smartville Road and plunging into the dense forests beyond. Hampered by insufficient light, they had great difficulty in following the trail, and by midnight had lost it entirely and were about ready to give up. Then another idea occurred to Mr. Hamer.

"I think that my old fox-hound would be able to pick up the trail," he told his companions. "Anyway, it's worth a try."

Acting upon the suggestion, young Schermerhorn returned to the Hamer farm and an hour or so later brought back the old hound. After a bit of circling the dog picked up the scent and set off through the woods, his bellows shattering the night stillness. The chase led in a circuitous route covering several miles and leading back toward the point of its origin; but finally the hunters knew by the hound's voice that the quarry had turned at bay.

Hurrying to the scene they found that a lively scrap was being waged by the bear and the dog in a dense thicket that rendered it very difficult to get a good view of the affair. Mr. Hamer grabbed the lantern and edged up as near as possible, hoping to get a shot.

"I wouldn't go too close, was I you, Tom," warned Huffstater nervously. "If he comes out of there he could kill you in a minute."

120

This Mr. Hamer knew to be true, but being of rugged pioneer stock he placed necessity before caution and continued to advance. Soon he was able to see clearly enough to get in a shot, and he fired both barrels of the rifle into the rearing black form that seemed much taller than a man. The bullets struck the animal in the neck, and it crashed out of the thicket and took refuge in a huge pile of hemlock tops some rods away, bleeding profusely.

The hound followed into the tangle, but after a brief skirmish in which he received several healthy cuffs, he decided that discretion was the best policy and retreated to help the hunters set up a guard about the pile until morning.

When daylight came the bear had lost a great amount of blood and was very weak, but still able to growl a savage defiance at the approach of the hunters. Two more bullets, this time in the head, ended the career of the old sheep-killer for all time, and the rejoicing but very tired hunters hauled their game out where they could really look it over.

It was then that they knew why the set-gun had only wounded instead of killing the animal. This bear was much above normal size, and the gun set to inflict a fatal body wound on a regular-sized animal had, of course, fired low and merely broken a front leg. Nevertheless, it had been the instrument of his downfall.

It was later found that the monster measured seven feet two and a half inches "from the tip of his nose to the tip of his toes," (quoting the newspaper extra) and although "spring poor," still weighed in at 370 pounds dressed. It was estimated that, if fat, he would have easily weighed 500 pounds.

Mr. Hamer loaded the carcass onto a wagon and drove into Lacona, about four miles away, where his advent caused much excitement. A bear of such proportions had never before been seen thereabouts, not even by the oldest hunters.

The meat, which in those days was considered a delicacy, was portioned out to friends and neighbors for their enjoyment. The magnificent, glossy black pelt was taken to the old Blodgett Tannery to be made into a robe. But unfortunately, before the robe was finished the building burned down; and thus Mr. Hamer lost forever the last memento of the famous Boylston Bear.

BUSH'S BEAR

The territory for quite a few miles on every side of Tug Hill used to be noted for its fish and game, and outstanding in the latter category were the many black bear that roamed the rugged hills and swamps. So numerous did these become that it got to be almost impossible for the owners of backwoods farms in the area to raise sheep, because of their mutton-hunting proclivities.

One old settler of Boyston township, on the western slope of the Hill, used to say that in early spring during the eighteen nineties the bears congregated so thickly around maple-syrup boiling places, and became so bold, that at night their eyes shone in the firelight, and they had to be driven away by banging on tin pans and flinging sticks of fire-wood. Knowing the black bear's love of anything sweet, and his ravenous appetite after coming out of hibernation, this seems to the writer to be very possible.

With the animals becoming such a nuisance, it became imperative that something should be done to reduce their numbers. As there were then no laws existing to protect the game, the farmers and woodsmen took matters into their own hands; tracking down and shooting the adults, and whenever possible, capturing the cubs alive for sale through agents to menageries and circuses.

This came to be quite a spring occupation, and put many badly needed dollars into the pockets of the hunters. Naturally, many became very adept at the business, and just as naturally, a great deal of rivalry developed among the more famous of this gentry.

Prominent among these was a short, stocky, sandy-haired individual by the name of John Bush; who killed his full share of the adult bears, and captured as many cubs as most hunters. But strange to relate, it was a bear that he did not kill which brought him the most fame.

Mr. Bush owned and operated a small farm up in the hills of east Boylston, and was skilled in many other things besides bear hunting; among these being trout fishing and the location of wild bee swarms. (He was also known for being an outspoken and vociferous Democrat in an almost complete Republican stronghold, but aside from shedding a little light on his makeup, this fact has no bearing on the story).

Like many another, he planned each year on adding to his income by spending the first weeks of April bear hunting. It was during this period that Bruin usually came out of hibernation, gaunt and hungry from a long winter's fast. It was also at this time that the females first brought out the new cubs, usually two in number, which had been born inside the den a few weeks before. These she took with her on her rambles in search of food, leaving a broad and easily followed trail in the snow.

Pleased indeed was the hunter who happened upon such a trail. With his snowshoes he could travel much more swiftly than the female bear encumbered by a pair of cubs, and usually it was not very long before he was pressing her closely.

When the hunter began to get dangerously close, she would force her offspring to climb some bushy evergreen where she believed they would escape detection; while she, unhindered now, would try to lure him away and elude him.

124

Coming upon the tree harboring the cubs, the hunter would tie a bransack around the trunk to prevent them from climbing down; after which he continued on after the mother bear, usually overtaking and killing her within a short time. With the pelt rolled into a bundle on his back, he would then go back and chop down the tree in which the cubs had taken refuge, pop them into the sack, and continue homeward. Pelts and live cubs were sold to various dealers who made periodic visits in the area for that purpose.

One morning early in April of 1912, Mr. Bush started out on such a hunting trip. After traveling for quite some time he came upon the trail of a sizeable bear wallowing through the deep snow, and as there were no accompanying cub tracks, he decided that it was either a male or farrow female. Soon he came to where the animal had attempted to cross Beaver Creek on the thaw-weakened ice and had fallen through, finally floundering out on the further bank.

Picking up the trail there, the hunter followed for another mile or so, suddenly coming upon the quarry almost immobilized in a drift. Ever since its immersion in the icy water, the animal's fur had continued to pick up snow which had frozen into ice balls, and these had now reached such a weight that he was barely able to flounder along.

No doubt the bear's weakened condition due to hunger and the icy bath also contributed to this result. Anyway, there he was, a good sized yearling but very subdued and docile, hardly able to growl his defiance as the hunter came upon him.

Mr. Bush was about to raise his 38/55 Winchester for the finishing shot when a brilliant thought struck him. Why not take the bear out alive? He knew that it was not more than a mile or so out to a farm owned by Roland Baigrie, on the Mad River road. If he could persuade the beast to go that far, it would be easy to get him the rest of the way home; and he would be worth much more money alive than dead. After a little thought and recourse to his Dutch ingenuity, he hit upon a plan which he decided was worth trying.

Unslinging his axe, he cut a pole about eight feet in length with a good solid crotch in one end, which he managed to manipulate over the back of the bear's neck. This he used as a steering medium, and also to foil an occasional half-hearted attempt at rebellion. Then by the dint of a good deal of pushing and shoving, aided by the liberal use of a long beech whip whenever necessary, believe it or not he drove that yearling bear out of the woods, across the clearing and right into the Baigrie woodshed.

With the game securely locked in, he walked the several miles home, where he harnessed his team to a sleigh, drove back, nailed the bear securely into a large wooden box, and proceeded to haul it home.

While the animal was half-starved and docile enough at first, his nature changed markedly after he became thoroughly thawed out and had been fed for a while. The writer, only a very small boy then, can vividly remember how he would glare and snarl as he paced back and forth behind the two-by-fours that had been nailed over the entrance to the box-stall in which he was kept; also how he would snap sticks in two with his teeth when they were poked through the bars.

After about two weeks a dealer from Lacona, by the name of William Turner, bought the animal and shipped him to a zoo in the mid-west.

Mr. Bush has been dead these many years, and while

126

he is remembered by many for widely diversified reasons, none excites more wonder than does his single-handed capture of Bush's Bear.

THE GREENFIELD
MURDER CASE

The moon, which during the two hours since it had risen, had been playing hide-and-seek among fast scudding clouds, finally slid behind a dense cloud bank and was lost to view. Almost immediately a thick but faintly luminous gloom settled down over the farms and forests of Orwell Township.

As if it had been waiting for just this to happen, a dark, silently gliding shadow detached itself from a clump of lilac bushes and stole toward the farmhouse. A vagrant moonbeam, escaping the clutches of the clouds for a brief moment, revealed that the shadowy form was human, and that it carried in its hand what appeared to be a stout club.

Without hesitation the prowler darted inside the unlocked door of the house. Very soon after, a listener on the outside might have heard the sound of sodden blows, followed by a slight scuffle and a half-strangled, gurgling cry.

Moments later, the dark figure of the intruder reappeared through the doorway, only now it carried no weapon in its hand. As silently as it had first appeared, it glided along the path toward the road and disappeared in the gloom. The rattling gurgle inside the house continued for two or three minutes, after which it ceased and all was still. As if it had now accomplished its devilish purpose, the errant moon slipped out of the clouds

129

and rode serene and high through the late October sky.

According to all documented evidence, thus began the affair known through the years as the Greenfield Murder Case, that was to rock the quiet countryside of Orwell Township in northeastern Oswego County. Later, its reverberations were to be felt throughout the state, even across the nation. Because of its bizarre implications, it was to be discussed and argued for years to come; a highly controversial case in which, many people contended, justice was really blindfolded by the court-room tactics of a brilliant prosecuting attorney.

The second scene in the drama opened at 3:15 A.M. on October 21, 1875, as William Grinnels, residing on the Orwell-Smartville road about two miles from Orwell Corners, was awakened by a rapping on his bedroom window.

"Who's there?" called Mr. Grinnels, instantly awake. The first thought that entered his mind concerned rumors of recent grain thefts in the immediate neighborhood.

"It's me, Orlando," answered a low voice. "I want you to get up and come with me. Hines has come to take Alice away."

Grinnels dressed swiftly and in a few moments stepped outside his door. He had recognized his nocturnal visitor as his nephew, Nathan Orlando Greenfield, who lived about eighty rods north along the road. By the light of the waning moon, he could see Greenfield hurrying along the road toward the house of his father, Richard Greenfield. This stood almost across the road, but a little south, of Orlando's own.

Hurrying to catch up, Grinnels had almost reached the house of the elder Greenfield when the latter joined his son on the road. There the two waited until Grinnels

130

came up, after which the three men went silently toward Orlando's house.

Here all was silent and dark, with no light showing anywhere. Going to the north side of the house, the men saw that the side kitchen door was slightly ajar.

"Orlando, this is your house, so you'd better go in first," whispered Grinnels. Greenfield made no reply, but pushed open the door and stepped inside. Almost immediately he came back out.

"There's no one in here," he announced. "I guess they've gone. Let's go to the barn . . . I want to see if there's been any more oats stole."

"Wait a minute," admonished Grinnels. "What has become of your wife Alice?"

"That's what I would like to know," returned Greenfield, starting along the path to the barn.

"Go inside and see if you can find your wife," commanded Grinnels. Greenfield came back and stepped inside the door again, and the two men could hear him stumbling about the dark kitchen. Suddenly his tense voice came out of the darkness.

"My god, I'll bet she's dead," they heard him gasp.

Immediately after there came a rasping of a match being struck, and a light flared up. Grinnels stepped swiftly into the room, to see Greenfield standing near an open door, match in hand, staring into the bedroom. Just then the match went out, but Grinnels had noted the location of a kerosene lamp on the table, and this he lighted. As he replaced the lamp-chimney and light flooded the room, the horror of the scene before him imprinted itself on a memory with a vividness that was never to fade.

Sprawled on the bedroom floor, just inside the door leading from the kitchen in which he stood, lay the still

131

form of Orlando's eighteen-year-old wife, Alice. The body lay partly on its side, partly on its face; the head slightly under the side of the bed; clad only in a torn and blood-stained nightgown. On the floor was a wide-spreading pool of blood, and more blood was spattered over the walls, the bedstead, the pillows, and the rumpled bed-clothing. Stepping closer, Grinnels saw that there was a gaping wound in the throat, from which dark blood still dribbled. Along the side of the face near the temple were two long, livid bruises, apparently caused by blows from some flat-sided weapon. Resting partly under the body lay what might well have been that very weapon: a three-foot length of hemlock edging about two inches wide.

All this time Greenfield had stood staring at the body of his wife, neither stirring a muscle or speaking a word. Suddenly he broke the silence.

"Oh look there," he said. "My gun is gone, too."

Taking him by the arm, Grinnels turned him around and guided him outside the house. Here he informed the elder Greenfield of what they had found, and the old man went inside to view the body briefly by the light of a lantern he had found.

"I think we should lift her up off the floor," were the next words that Orlando spoke, but Grinnels vetoed this.

"No, we mustn't touch anything until the coroner comes," he said.

Shortly after, Grinnels suggested that they should call some of the other neighbors to the scene, but when he and the elder Greenfield started to act on the suggestion, Orlando seemed terror-stricken.

"Please don't leave me here alone," he begged, so his father stayed with him while Grinnels hurried away, to return shortly after with Leman Greenfield, a cousin who lived nearby, and Elbert Stowell, another neighbor.

132

Leaving the two neighbors with the father and son, Grinnels then went to his own barn, where he hitched a horse to a buggy and hurried away to summon Coroner David A. Lawton and the local constable, a man by the name of Abner Dillenbeck. It was well after daylight when the three arrived back at the Greenfield farm.

By this time quite a crowd of curious neighbors had arrived and were standing about, but to all appearances, nothing had been touched when the coroner took over the investigation.

The first thing the official noticed upon entering the kitchen was the form of a small child lying on a couch covered by a blanket, where she had slept peacefully all night within a few feet of her murdered mother. The little girl was removed and taken to the home of her grandparents across the road.

The coroner then began a detailed examination of the dead body. He found the body itself warm, but the limbs cold with no signs of rigor mortis as yet. After a careful examination, and various measurements had been made, he had the body removed to the kitchen, where it was placed on the couch and covered.

He then turned his attention to a minute inspection of the murder room, paying particular heed to the size, shape, and position of the various spots and smears of blood. The hemlock club that had lain beneath the body was carefully examined, and was found to be broken almost in two by the exertion of great force, conceivably the striking of blows. It was found to be covered with blood, and several of the victim's hairs adhered to it.

In that day and age, the science of finger-printing had not been perfected in this country, so no attention was paid to this possible source of valuable evidence.

A thorough search of the entire house was then instituted by the coroner and Constable Dillenbeck, but nothing of importance was turned up until they came to the buttery (pantry). There, on a high shelf, they discovered a large pocket-knife with a blade nearly four inches long. The large blade was open and the whole knife was smeared with what appeared to be blood. This the coroner carefully wrapped and took with him.

Later in the morning a careful search was made of the immediate vicinity of the house and barn by the constable and several neighbors. Two tread-down spots that appeared to have been made by a person standing there for some time were discovered; one in the road a few rods north of the Greenfield house, the other at the side of the front yard, near some lilac bushes. These were fenced off to preserve them for the inspection of District Attorney John J. Lamoree, who had been sent for. On the sand of the path leading from the kitchen door to the road were discovered several spatters of blood.

A diligent searcher who went farther afield than the others, reported that there were blood spots on the well-curb near Richard Greenfield's house; and more on the back door of that house, near the knob. Hurrying across the road, the coroner discovered this to be so.

As the morning progressed, the coroner and Constable Dillenbeck began to hear certain snatches of conversation among groups of people clustered about that seemed to direct a great deal of suspicion toward the husband of the murdered woman. It was common knowledge that there had been much marital friction in the Greenfield household for some time, and that the dead woman had on several occasions voiced her intentions of leaving her husband. It was rumored that she had been "carrying on" with several men in the community, and with one young man in particular; that Orlando was very

134

jealous; that he had threatened to shoot said young man if he found him at his house again; that he had threatened to kill his wife; that he had beat and kicked her on several occasions. One man said that Orlando had made the remark soon after his wife's mother's funeral, "Alice will be lying beside her in the graveyard within two months."

Just how much of this talk might be true, Coroner Lawton had no way of knowing, so to be on the safe side he quietly told Constable Dillenbeck to keep the man under constant surveillance.

A great deal of unfavorable comment was also elicited by the apparent lack of remorse displayed by Orlando toward his wife's death, and the absence of any trace of tenderness or sorrow. He seemed to place much more importance on the fact that his double-barreled shotgun was missing, and that someone had allegedly stolen fifteen or twenty bushels of oats from his barn.

Upon arriving at the scene, one neighbor said to him, "This is a bad thing, Orlando;" upon which he replied, "Yes, I have lost twenty bushels of oats." Another neighbor by the name of Hiram Snow, who was known to have a good deal of knowledge concerning law, was approached by Greenfield, who said to him, "What should I do about getting a search warrant to find my oats?" Mr. Snow answered him, "Never mind about your oats until we have found out who murdered this poor woman."

By the time District Attorney Lamoree arrived on the scene at about 9 A.M., feeling was beginning to run high against not only Orlando, but most of the Greenfield clan as well. At nine-thirty a coroner's jury was convened in the house of Richard Greenfield, across the road, and this somewhat relieved the tension.

During this session, Orlando was questioned con-

135

cerning his whereabouts on the night before, and told a strange story. He said that he had spent the day before threshing grain in the company of Charles Myers at a farm owned by Joseph Wyman, a few miles away. At about eight o'clock that evening he had started to walk home. When about thirty rods from his house he had met a team and wagon driven by George Hines, who lived not far away, and as he was somewhat doubtful of Hines' honesty, had stopped behind a tree to let the wagon go on past.

Asked how he could tell in the darkness that it was Hines' wagon outfit, he replied that he had sold the wagon to Hines and recognized the peculiar rattling that it made.

After the wagon had passed he followed along behind, not letting his presence be known. Upon reaching home, Hines set about putting his horses in the barn, which gave Greenfield an opportunity to examine the contents of the wagon. He said it contained oats in bags, about fifteen or twenty bushels of them so far as he could tell.

Orlando said that he then cut cross-lots to his own home, arriving there about eleven o'clock. He went immediately into his barn, where he discovered that several bushels of oats in bags were missing, and another several bushels gone from the bin.

He said that he then went into his house, to find his wife in bed. He asked her who had been there, and she replied that nobody had. He said, "I guess there has been . . . there are twenty bushels of oats missing." His wife then admitted that George Hines had been there that evening, but said that he had not taken away any oats.

Orlando then asked her if it was her intention to leave him, and she replied, "Yes, George Hines is coming

136

back later in the night to take me to live at Charley Grinel's house."

Upon hearing this, Orlando stated, he immediately left the house and went across the road to his father's residence. Here he aroused his father from sleep, related to him what had happened, and asked him to go and see for himself that oats had been stolen. The elder man dressed, lighted a lantern, and the two returned to Orlando's barn.

After visiting the barn the two men entered the house again. The elder Greenfield sat down in the kitchen while his son entered the bedroom, sat down on the side of the bed, and started talking to his wife.

He asked her if it would be necessary for her to pay her board where she was going, and she replied that it would not be.

"What do you think we should do about the children?" (there were three, with another expected in a few months) he then asked her, and her answer was, "I don't know, and don't care, either." He then stood up, and he and his father went back across the road to his parents' home again. There he undressed and went to bed with his older brother, Ezra. (These statements were verified by the older man.)

"Why didn't you spend the night at your own home with your wife?" the coroner asked him.

"Because I was afraid," returned Orlando.

"Afraid of what?" asked the coroner.

"I was afraid that if anything happened to my wife it would be laid against me," stated Greenfield.

Going on with his story, he related that he had not been able to get to sleep. His brother had awakened and they had talked for a time. Later, he had heard one of his children crying downstairs. The child had been quieted by its grandmother. He had heard a door slam on the piazza downstairs. Quite a while later, still unable to sleep because of his problems, he had risen from bed and stood gazing out of the window toward his own house. He then noticed that there was a light in the house.

Dressing swiftly, he went across the road toward his place, not going nearer than two or three rods of the house, he stated. Here he could see through the window a man whom he thought he recognized as George Hines, with a lantern in his hand. Going back across the road, Orlando knocked on his father's window to reawaken him, and then hurried up the road to the home of his uncle, William Grinnell, whom he awakened and asked to accompany him. He said that when he came opposite the house of his father, who was dressed and awaiting them, he noticed that the light in his own house was now out. The three of them had gone to the house, entered, and discovered the body of his wife.

When asked to explain the presence of blood-spots on the pathway from his house, and on his father's well-curb, he said that he could not do so. He readily admitted that the bloodstained knife found by the coroner belonged to him, but when questioned about the blood on it he told three conflicting stories. One was that he had cut his finger while trying to remove a sliver; another that his brother Ezra had borrowed the knife to cut off turnip tops and had gashed his hand badly. The third was that he had used the knife to butcher a lamb for his father several days before, and had placed it on a shelf uncleaned.

Several other witnesses were heard by the coroner's jury, giving testimony relating to the marital troubles in the Greenfield household, also threats and remarks alleged to have been made by the husband. All this was, of course, very damaging to Orlando, and the outcome of the session became increasingly plain. When the group finally concluded their duties at about nine-thirty in the evening, it took them only a few minutes to reach a verdict.

Alice Greenfield, they ruled, had met her death by willful homicide; presumably at the hands of her husband, Nathan Orlando Greenfield. A warrant was immediately issued and he was placed under arrest by Constable Dillenbeck.

During the last few hours of the inquest, a wave of resentment against Orlando had steadily been growing, fanned by the activities and inflammatory remarks of several members of the hot-headed younger element of the community. By the time that the findings of the coroner's jury were made known, this feeling had reached fever pitch. When the arrest was affected, the prisoner's mother remarked that it was too bad that he must go away without being able to settle up his threshing accounts, and that he should be allowed to come back in a few days to settle up.

Hearing this, one young man from Boylston shouted, "Yes, let him come back and we'll settle his accounts once and for all." At that, an angry crowd began to mill about, and someone shouted, "Get a rope."

Seeing the dangerous trend of affairs, the coroner and constable at once placed the prisoner in a light wagon and rushed him to the jail in Pulaski, several miles away, for safe-keeping.

During the days and weeks that followed, a staggering amount of evidence was amassed against Greenfield. A post-mortem examination of the body had established the fact that the two blows on the victim's head would have produced a stunning effect but would

139

was a taciturn and unpredictable man, subject to sudden and violent bursts of temper, that he had been cruel and inhuman toward his wife, that he was exceedingly jealous of her, and had made many threats of bodily harm against both her and certain young men whom he believed had been paying her attentions, that he had beat and kicked her on occasions, and had even locked her out of her home a few days before her death.

The district attorney pointed out that the murdered wife had been married to the defendant while virtually a child, and that with three children on her hands she had little choice but to go on living with him and accepting whatever treatment he accorded her.

He introduced witnesses to the hitherto unknown fact that several bags of oats, presumably those alleged to have been stolen from the Greenfield property, were later found hidden beneath hay and straw in the Greenfield barn. He advanced the theory that Orlando himself had placed them there in an effort to cover up his own guilt by the implication that the scene of the crime had been visited by another party or parties bent on mischief.

He attempted to establish the fact that Orlando, as well as nearly every member of the Greenfield clan, was dishonest and unreliable, and that the word of any of them could not be accepted even under oath. His efforts to establish the knife as the murder weapon, and connect its use with the prisoner, were artfully conducted and had an appearance of great authenticity, even though they were wholly circumstantial.

It was his contention that the accused man had committed the foul murder, gone to the pump behind his father's house, washed the bloodstains from his person and as much of his clothing as possible, disposed of more of his clothing, and then awoke his father and Grinels to witness the finding of the body. The prosecution's case was completed on June 14th and Judge Huntington and his aides took over for the defense.

However able had been the handling of the case by the district attorney, Judge Huntington's was none-the-less so. Displaying an easy familiarity with medical analysis and terminology, he went on to prove that Dr. Richardson's methods of blood analysis were bungling and obsolete, thus impeaching much of the evidence that had been offered regarding the stains on the alleged murder weapon. He pointed out that, while the crime must have been committed by someone familiar with the butchering of animals, this fact would apply to nearly every man for miles around as well as the prisoner. He stressed the contention that many other persons might have had opportunities and even motives equal to those of the prisner, for the commission of the crime.

For every witness for the prosecution who had testified regarding the unfeeling brutality and general unreliability of Greenfield and his relatives, he produced a character witness who attested to the fact that he had always enjoyed a good reputation, that he was honest and reliable, that he was hard-working, thrifty, and temperate, that he had never been seen to display brutality or meanness toward his wife and children, that he had never been heard to threaten bodily harm, either against them or anyone else.

By the testimony of Ezra Greenfield, brother of the accused, he brought out the fact that the stains on the door of their father's house had been left there when he, Ezra, had cut his hand while trimming turnips; and that the supposed bloodstains on the well-curb were not blood at all, but spots of red paint left there by the cleaning of paint brushes.

143

He pointed to the absence of blood on the prisoner's clothing when apprehended, stating that the murderer's clothes must have been liberally spattered. Orlando, he said, had never attempted to escape from the murder scene as a guilty man might do, and had made no attempt to hide the knife claimed by the prosecution to be the murder weapon. He had offered ready and unprompted testimony concerning his actions, his marital troubles, and his relations with his wife. In point of fact, his whole demeanor had never resembled the actions of a guilty man.

In rebuttal of the surprise testimony regarding the hidden bags of grain, the defense attorney advanced the theory that there was no sound evidence that the grain had in fact been placed there by Orlando; that it might as well been placed there by someone wishing to add to the web of circumstantial evidence that had enmeshed the defendant. He pointed out that the shotgun alleged to have been stolen at the same time as the grain had never been found, and slyly hinted at the fact that a shotgun has readily identifiable characteristics not found in a sack of oats, which, after all, looks pretty much like another sack of oats.

Judge Huntington offered the probability that the crime had been committed by a person or persons unknown, probably a wandering tramp or ravisher, and that a series of unfortunate coincidences had cast a mantle of guilt and suspicion upon the prisoner.

Late in the evening of the twenty-fifth day of the trial, after having been charged at length by Judge Noxon concerning their duties as an instrument of justice, the jury received the case and retired to the jury room to give it their consideration. After thirty-six hours of deliberation they returned to the courtroom to announce that they were in hopeless disagreement, with no hope of reaching a verdict. Accordingly, they were dismissed and the prisoner was ordered held for a second trial.

From then until early in the next year, Greenfield was held in the county jail at Oswego, where he proved to be a model prisoner. In fact, he came to be quite popular with the jailers who had him in charge, and with the reporters who came from far and wide to interview him. During this period he also embraced religion, a factor that had never hitherto entered into his life. During all this time he steadfastly protested his innocence.

The second trial officially began on February 13, 1877, but, as in the case of the first, the selection of the jury required three days, so it was not until February sixteenth that presentation of evidence began. Again John L. Lamoree represented the prosecution and the Hon. S. C. Huntington acted for the defense, but this time Hon. M. H. Merwin acted as the presiding justice.

In this trial virtually no new evidence was presented by either side, and the proceedings largely followed the pattern of the year before. On March first the case was placed in the hands of the jury, who deliberated until the next day, when they returned a verdict of guilty of murder in the first degree.

The sentencing was deferred until March nineteenth. At two o'clock in the afternoon the prisoner was again brought before the judge, who said,

"Greenfield, stand up."

The prisoner arose, and the judge continued,

"Greenfield, you have been tried and found guilty of the murder of your wife, Alice. Have you anything to say why the death sentence should not be pronounced upon you?"

"I have, your honor," Greenfield replied. "I am not

145

guilty, and I call upon God, by who I expect to be judged, to witness it."

"The judgement of this court," Judge Merwin went on grimly, "is that you be taken to the Oswego County Jail, where you will be securely confined until Friday, the eleventh of May, and that on that day, between the hours of 10 A.M. and 4 P.M., either in the jail or in the yard adjacent thereto, you be hung by the neck until you are dead. May God have mercy on your soul."

This sentence was in due time carried out, but not to the letter. Since Oswego County had no facilities for an execution, the prisoner was transferred to the Onondaga County Jail in Syracuse. There he was, in fact, hanged by the neck until dead, in the prison yard of the old penitentiary on the north side, where a high school was later erected. His was the unenviable distinction of being the last person executed by hanging in the State of New York.

The prisoner's body was claimed by his father, who hauled it back to its native hills in a lumber wagon. Here it was placed in an unmarked grave beneath an apple tree, back of the old home where Orlando had been raised. It is said that for many months after the burial a lighted lantern was hung on the lower branch of the tree to discourage grave-robbers and curiosity seekers.

However this may be, the argument concerning the guilt or innocence of Nathan Orlando Greenfield waxed unabated for many years among his acquaintances, and is still discussed among the older residents of the area.

PRANKS...
AND PRANKSTERS

However numerous might have been the qualities and assets lacked by the rural and backwoods communities throughout the Tug Hill territory, certainly one of these was not a sense of humor. In the old days this was one commodity that was cherished, nurtured, and developed above all others.

Sources of amusement were few and far between. Television, radio, and motion pictures were unheard of; even the new-fangled "talking machines" were exceedingly scarce and limited to the ownership of the rich or near-rich. Books and magazines were fairly easy to come by, but it must be remembered that among rural folks in those days, only a privileged few could read or write to any extent. Upon these few devolved the duty of passing on to the others whatever measure of knowledge and entertainment might be derived from such sources.

Thus it became common practice for the male population of a community to meet at every leisure opportunity; in little informal gatherings at taverns, blacksmith shops, cross-roads stores, and post-offices. The main objects of these get-togethers was the gathering and dispensing of news and the search for amusement.

A good story-teller with a large stock of humorous anecdotes was always popular and something to be treasured in a community. And any new prank or happening that gave the people something to discuss and laugh about was valued highly and kept fresh and green by repeated telling.

Many of these tricks and pranks were genuinely spontaneous, spur-of-the-moment affairs. Others were carefully planned by practical jokers in the tiniest detail; sometimes days or weeks in advance, and awaiting only a suitable opportunity for their fulfillment.

To some readers, especially those of the younger generation, many of these happenings may seem of trivial interest, and to contain only a mediocre degree of humor. This is because they can judge only by the somewhat more sophisticated standards of the present day. As many an old-timer can testify, life three-quarters of a century ago was much more simple than in modern times. Likewise, the old-time sense of humor was vastly more simple and direct, and thus more easily satisfied, than it is today.

It is probable that every rural community throughout the country could produce its own collection of amusing doings, which have kept folks entertained and laughing down through the years. Only a few of the ones pertinent to the Tug Hill country can be mentioned here.

* * * * * *

A group of young men from Boylston and North Redfield had walked to the twin villages of Lacona and Sandy Creek, to enjoy a Saturday evening of entertainment and camaraderie, at the many gathering places there. All during the evening they continued to come into contact with a certain citizen of the nearby village of Smartville, who was making the rounds of the drinking places and imbibing rather more than was good for him.

The youths tried admonishing the older man to take

148

it a little easy on the liquor, but each time he good-naturedly brushed aside their warnings and went merrily on his way, taking on a heavier and heavier load. At last he disappeared.

Some time after midnight the young men were on their way home to bed, walking the Lacona-Boylston road by the light of a waning moon. Some three miles out of town their attention was attracted by a sound coming from an angle formed where three stone walls came together. Peering cautiously in, they could dimly make out the figure of a man lying in there, rolling about as though in great pain.

Lighting a match they immediately recognized the man as the one from Smartville who had been doing the heavy drinking all evening. A hasty examination showed them that he was not injured, and they decided that he was merely sleeping off his jag, his slumber being attended by bad dreams.

The night was a rather chilly one to leave the man lying out on the ground, so the young men agreed that it would be necessary to sober him up and get him home to bed. For their own comfort as well as his, they rounded up a few armfuls of wood and started a roaring fire in the fence angle, which soon lighted up the surrounding trees and stone-walls with a ruddy glow.

Soon the heat from the fire coupled with repeated shakings began to have their effect on the inebriated man, and he opened his eyes to what must have seemed to him a Satanic scene. Fire and smoke all around him, and the heat becoming more and more intense. With a startled gasp he sat bolt upright, suddenly well on his way to sobriety.

"Where in hell am I?" was the first question he put

149

to the shadowy figures squatting around, whom he recognized as acquaintances.

"That's just where you are . . . in Hell . . . sent here for getting drunk once too often," returned one of the youths in a sepulchural tone.

The man considered this bit of information soberly for a moment.

"Just as I figured," he said at last. "Tell me . . . how long have you boys been here?"

"We've been here for two weeks," someone answered. "Why, what difference does it make?"

"Well, you're better acquainted around here than I am," said the man from Smartville. "You just lead the way to a good place and I'll buy the drinks for the crowd."

*　*　*　*　*　*

Up in Lorraine in the old days, Ezra Bellinger used to run a barber shop in part of an old mill that stood on the bank of Sandy Creek, which bisects the village. This shop was a favorite meeting place for the male citizens of the community, who gathered there to gossip and play cards or checkers. Sometimes these sessions ran far, far into the night.

This was alright with Ez, who enjoyed the fun as well as anyone. But during cold weather it took a lot of wood to feed the old pot-bellied stove for such long periods of time. One evening Ez told the boys that if they were going to continue to use his place, they would have to help furnish the fuel.

This plan was readily agreed to by the card and checker players, who allowed that it was no more than fair. From then on, each man or boy carried in a huge armful of wood when he arrived for the nightly session. Soon the supply began to exceed the demand, and a sur-

150

plus started to build up. Sly old Ezra grinned to himself, thinking that he had the problem licked.

But after a while he began to notice that his own supply of wood, cut and carefully piled in his woodshed the summer before, was diminishing at an alarming rate. This aroused his suspicions, and he decided to investigate.

One evening, just as the usual congregation was beginning to arrive, Ez slipped quietly from his shop and secreted himself in his woodshed. Soon the door opened and one of the checker players slipped quietly inside, loaded his arms with wood, and departed for the barbershop. He was followed by another and another, who did the same.

Ezra had seen enough. Never one to fail to appreciate a good joke, even when it was on himself, he was inwardly grinning to himself when he went back to the shop and confronted the men with the knowledge he had gained.

"Why yes," drawled one of the man. "You told us we had to furnish the wood, but you never told us where we had to get it."

*　　*　　*　　*　　*　　*

When Larry Meeghan reached advanced years and retired from the rigorous life of a lumberman and river-boss, he was moderately well-to-do and decided to invest his money in the pursuit of agriculture. Accordingly, he went up into the hills of Boylston and bought a large tract of woodland which he had looked over and decided had the potential of good farming land.

Into this he took a gang of men, cutting and burning the waste timber and brush, pulling or burning the stumps, and creating in the forest what was known for years as Meeghan's Clearing. Here he built an impressive array of barns and farm buildings and a fine house, using lumber sawed from the large amount of timber on his holdings. Inside of a very few years his progessive vision and untiring ambition had won for him a very large and productive farm in the wilderness, employing several men, and connected with the old Military Highway by a well-kept private road.

In those days mowing machines and hayrakes were practically unknown. Hay and grain were harvested with scythes and handrakes, and loaded onto wagons with pitchforks. During haying season Larry made a practice of hiring several extra hands to do this added work.

One summer during haying, a young boy in his teens came to Larry's place in search of a job. Noting the lad's ragged and underfed appearance, Larry took pity on him him and hired him, figuring he could find something for the boy to do.

"One thing you've got to understand," he told the lad the first morning, when the day's work was about to begin. "When I put a man on a job, I like to have him stick to it until I put him on another one. Just you remember that."

The young man allowed that he would stick to any job that he was placed on, and Larry put him to turning a large grindstone, on which the mowers were grinding their scythes.

Later in the day, Meeghan started out on a cattle-buying trip, leaving the haying operations in the capable hands of his farm boss. Making his preparations to leave, he completely forgot the youth whom he had recently hired.

Two days later he returned from the trip. Going out toward the barns, the first thing his eyes encountered

152

was the youth, seated on a box and patiently turning the grindstone, even though there was not a scythe or mower anywhere in sight.

"What the devil do you think you're doing, boy?" exploded Larry.

"Turning the grindstone, Mr. Meeghan, just like you told me to," returned the youth, never pausing a moment.

"You mean to say you've been twistin' that thing for two days?" asked Larry, unbelieving.

"Yes sir, you never told me to stop yet," said the boy.

"Well, you can stop now," said Larry, realizing that what the boy said was the truth.

"Gosh, that's sure good news," returned the boy. "You know, Mr. Meeghan, this job was startin' to get a little tiresome."

Later, Larry learned from his farm boss that the lad had, indeed, turned the grindstone for two days; pausing only for meals and quitting when the grinding was done for the night. Each morning he was back at it bright and early. The fact that most of the time there were no scythes to be ground made no difference to him.

The grinning farm boss said he had tried to explain to the boy that he was supposed to turn the stone only when there was grinding to be done, only to be informed that "Mr. Meeghan put me on this job and he'll tell me when to stop."

In later years Larry derived a great deal of amusement out of telling this tale, and "Stick to your grindstone" became a favorite slogan of his.

* * * * * *

Many years ago there lived on the western slope of Tug Hill, near the village of Worth, an extremely picturesque and eccentric old lady by the name of Sophronia Laisure.

153

Sometime during her youth, some illness or other unfortunate incident had caused a mild mental derangement which had remained with her throughout her life, rendering her what people referred to in those days as "a little queer." While some of the exploits and sayings credited to her seem to indicate that the moniker did not exactly fit her, she became known as "Crazy Sophrone."

Sophronia never married, but earned her living working as a hired woman in some of the more well-to-do homes. Due to her industry and skill as a housekeeper, as well as a spinner and weaver, her services were always in great demand, in spite of her affliction. With her earnings she managed to maintain her own small house, so she could always "have a place to go to."

Oftentimes she would embark on long and extended trips, tramping the highway from Barnes Corners to Osceola, and west sometimes as far as Lake Ontario. She presented a picturesque figure indeed as she strode along, clad in handed-down clothing and with her neck festooned with necklaces made from colored buttons strung on twine, chanting strange little songs and incantations.

People said that she vaguely resembled a witch, and many of the superstitious feared her as such. But most folks recognized her for what she really was, a good-natured old eccentric with an itchy foot and a desire to see far distant places and faces.

One time she entered a store in Mannsville, intent upon making a purchase. Marching up to a young man who was working there as clerk, she announced that she wanted to buy five yards of Turkey-red muslin.

When the clerk went to get the material, he discovered that the store was entirely out of muslin of the color desired, but believing the old lady to be mildly demented, he suspected that it would be an easy task to palm off an equal amount of another color. Without asking her permission he took down a bolt of bright blue cloth and started to measure off the desired amount.

"Just a minute, young man," said Sophronia. "I ordered red, not blue."

"Now Aunt Sophrony," cajoled the clerk. "This is just what you want. You just imagine that it is red, and it will be red."

"Why, that's right," agreed the old woman readily. "I never thought about it like that before. I'll take it."

With a self-satisfied smirk the young man measured off the desired yardage, inwardly thinking how very easy it was to put something over on the old lady. Sophronia picked up the package, thanked him politely, and started to walk out of the store.

"Just a minute, Aunt Sophroney," called the clerk. "You ain't paid me yet."

"Well, you just imagine that you've been paid for this blue cloth that I imagine is red, and you will be paid," returned Sophronia calmly, and walked out.

* * * * * *

For many years, right up until Prohibition went into effect during the first quarter of the twentieth century, it was possible to buy unadulterated grain alcohol in most any hotel, saloon, or drugstore in the country. By this I mean in any of the towns in which the citizens had exercised their right to local option and voted the town "wet" instead of "dry."

This colorless and extremely potent liquid, known as alky, was highly regarded by many people for its alleged medicinal properties, and few households failed to keep a bottle on hand for use in hot slings and toddies, in case of a cold or chills. It has been said that many a blue-nosed old church deacon who would rather be

155

found dead than caught taking a drink, often imagined convenient ailments as an excuse to get a legitimate sample of the forbidden fruit.

To the drinking element of the population it had quite another value. When reduced somewhat with water from its natural breath-strangling state, it made quite a potable beverage, especially when flavored with a little burnt sugar or lemon juice. Some of the leather-throated old lumberjacks were even known to partake of it in its uncut form, but this was not generally the case.

Most saloon and hotel-keepers kept a barrel of alky behind the bar, from which they could fill bottles brought in by their customers, thus keeping the price as low as possible.

This custom was followed by the keeper of the Ben Lewis House in Redfield, a famous old hostelry which still stands in that historic village. One day, a good many years ago, there came to the hotel a man well known to the proprietor as being a moderate drinker and an honest, if not too prosperous, fellow. This man brought with him two quart bottles which he asked to have filled with alky.

The hotel-keeper did as requested, after which the man said to him, "You'll have to trust me for this for a few days. I don't have the money to pay for it right now."

"Why, that's alright," said the hotel-keeper, who had no fears on that score. He entered the sale in his credit-book and the man thanked him, took his bottles, and left the inn.

Within half an hour he was back, still carrying the two quart bottles, which he set on the bar.

"I've thought it over and decided that I can't afford to spend money for liquor," he told the hotel man. "Might better buy a sack of flour to feed my children. Take my name off your book."

156

This was a very wise and commendable attitude, the hotel-keeper had to admit, and he readily crossed out the charge against the man. The two bottles he placed aside, being too busy at the moment to empty their contents back into the barrel.

Some time later the hotel was visited by another customer who told an amusing tale of seeing the man in another part of the village, roaring drunk and urging everyone he met to have a drink with him from the two quarts of alcohol that he carried.

This set the Ben Lewis proprietor to wondering about the fellow's abrupt change of heart, and a suspicion that he had been swindled began to form in his mind. Remembering that the two bottles which had been returned were still untouched, he emptied a small portion from one into a glass and tasted it. It had an alcohol smell and taste alright, but a very weak one, to say the least.

It was not until some time later that the hotel-man learned for sure what had happened, and the joke was so good that he couldn't keep it to himself. Immediately after leaving the hotel, the customer had gone to the town pump, where he had a couple of other bottles secreted. Into these he had poured most of the alcohol, leaving only enough to give the water with which he refilled the original bottles a pungent smell and taste.

These he had returned to the unsuspecting proprietor, believing that they would be emptied back into the barrel and the fraud would go undiscovered ... while he went his merry way enjoying a free drunk.

*   *   *   *   *   *

Back in the days when Ed Moore first started to operate a general store in Lorraine Huddle, he made a practice, in accordance with a custom followed by Frank Overton, Olin Reed, and other merchants of the village,

157

of keeping a large glass jar of smoking tobacco sitting on a counter in a conspicuous place.

This was usually Warnicky (Warnick & Brown), Growler (with the large bulldog's head displayed on the yellow package), or Corn Cake; three brands of unadulterated strength and definite aroma usually favored by the smokers of the community. It was kept there for the convenience of the many farmers, lumbermen, and townsmen who regularly patronized the store, and who liked to fill their pipes with free tobacco when they came inside to trade or gossip.

At this time one of the citizens of the town was an old gentleman with a very small income and a very large appetite for the solace of the pipe. People thought it rather curious that, although he was seldom seen without a large corncob pipe in his mouth, he was never known to purchase smoking tobacco in any of the stores. Although he made the rounds each day of the establishments furnishing free tobacco, filling his pipe in each one, it did not seem that this should keep him in continuous supply.

One day when he stood stuffing the old corncob in Mr. Moore's store, the merchant noticed that it seemed to take him an unusually long time. On subsequent days, Mr. Moore kept surreptitious watch, and at last discovered the secret of the old gentleman's tobacco supply.

It seemed that the old schemer had bored a hole clear through the bottom of the pipe, which he had then closed with a readily removable plug. On going into a store he would remove the plug, palm the pipe, and proceed to stuff tobacco right through it until his hand was full. This he would place in his pocket on pretext of reaching for a match, after which the plug was slipped back in and the pipe lighted. By visiting several stores

158

a day he thus enjoyed a steady and unending supply of smoking.

This mild form of larceny was winked at by Mr. Moore and the other Lorraine merchants, who had many a laugh over it but never mentioned it to the venerable old free-loader. He, in his turn, probably enjoyed many a secret chuckle over the ingenuity of his ruse.

JOKES . . .
AND JOKESTERS

Like the pranks that were played in the old days, that lived on down through the years to create such merriment in the retelling, so were jokes and sly sayings repeated and treasured.

Most of these sayings were absolutely spontaneous and unplanned, not designed or intended to attract more than passing notice. After all, this seems to be one of the standards by which true humor is measured. Many were synchronized to the day and age in which they were spoken, and couched in terms of those days. These could not possibly be appreciated by members of later generations, and have been sorted out and omitted. But following are a few of the ones that should tickle almost anyone's funny-bone.

* * * * * *

Jim Dailey was employed by the Blount Lumber Company in the erection of a huge saw-mill in the forests of Boylston. Jim was working with several other men on a staging fastened to the side of the structure, when the staging for some reason started to fall down.

"The damned mill is fallin' away from us, boys," Jim yelled. "But just hang on to the scaffold and let 'er go."

* * * * * *

Larry Meeghan had hired a young fellow to work on his farm, helping with the chores and doing odd jobs around the place. It was winter, and therefor very dark yet, when Larry roused the young man at about four o'clock the first morning. When he came downstairs the youth was dressed in his best clothes and carried his satchel in his hand.

"Where do you think you're goin', young feller?" asked Larry, thinking him to be still half asleep.

"Goin' to find a place to stay all night," returned the youth, as he walked out the door.

* * * * * *

Amos Ridgeway, who lived for years in the Boylston hills and gained much fame for his sparkling wit as well as for his amazing insight into rural law, owned a large and very ugly hog which he had kept around for several years.

"Why don't you butcher that hog, Amos?" a neighbor asked him one day. "Why have you kept it around so long?"

"Well, it's this way," answered Amos. "I've got to keep *some* hog around, seein' as how I've got a farm, and it might as well be that one, now that he's got used to me."

* * * * * *

When Amos had reached an age of almost a hundred, his eyesight began to fail to such an extent that he could no longer shave himself. This chore was then taken over by one of his sons.

One day, while shaving the old gentleman, the younger man made a slip and nicked Amos' skin with the razor.

"Gosh, Dad, you sure nick easy," commented the son. "Must be your skin is awfully thin."

"Well, boy," grinned the old man, "you wear your skin as long as I have mine and yours'll be thin, too."

* * * * * *

A school-meeting was in session in what was known

162

as the Phelps District, in upper Boylston. The erection of a new schoolhouse was the issue being voted upon, and when the votes had been counted it was found that the motion to build had been carried almost unanimously.

At this point a thrifty but well-meaning taxpayer arose and made a suggestion that the old schoolhouse should be torn down and the material used in the construction of the new one.

"But where will we hold school in the meantime?" someone asked.

"Why," said the first man disgustedly, "we'll use the old school until the new one is ready, of course."

* * * * * *

Teasel's Tavern used to stand between Orwell and Altmar, at that time called Sandbanks, and was at one time a well-patronized hostelry. It was owned and run by Orvil Teasel, a jolly and robust individual who loved a joke as well as the next fellow; no matter who the joke was on.

One cold autumn evening a nondescript sort of fellow came into the bar-room, seeking free board and lodging for the night.

"Well, now," said Mr. Teasel, "I'll be glad to set up a drink, but I'm afraid I can't afford to furnish free board and lodging for everyone who asks for it. Folks usually work for them things."

"Well, I ain't very good at work," returned the stranger. "Got shot up in the war and ain't been worth much since."

"Seems too bad to let an old veteran sleep out in the cold," remarked one of the several patrons in the barroom.

"Well, yes it does," agreed Teasel, "Ain't there any-

163

thing that you can do to earn your night's lodging, mister?"

"About the only thing that I can do well is make up poetry," returned the man.

"Now there you are," exclaimed Teasel, sensing a chance to create a little entertainment for his patrons. "Now I'm sure to be dieing one of these days, and so far I ain't got a danged verse for my tombstone. You write me an epitaph and I'll give you a night's board and lodging."

"I'll write half of it now," agreed the man, displaying a canny distrust of the honesty of inn-keepers. "And if you like it, you let me stay tonight and I'll write the other half in the morning."

This seemed reasonable to Teasel, who agreed, and handed the stranger a pencil and paper. In a remarkably short time the man had produced this rhyme:
> "Here lies a man who died of late,
>   And was borne by angels to Heaven's gate..."

This pleased the inn-keeper very much, and he furnished the poet with supper and a bed, and breakfast the next morning. After breakfast, he said to the man,

"Well, it's time for the other half of the epitaph."

"The bed was lumpy and the vittles wasn't none too good," remarked the poet.

"Now don't go trying to back out of your agreement," said Teasel, thrusting paper and pencil toward the fellow.

"Oh, I'll stick to my bargain, alright," said the poet, and taking up the pencil he wrote the other half of the verse, as follows:
> "Then up stepped the Devil, as sly as a weasel,
>   And down into Hell he pitched old Teasel."

Another epitaph for a tombstone, this time his own, was composed by Henry Moore, who lived in the Town of Lorraine years ago and was well known for his poeti-

164

cal abilities. The epitaph, said to have been actually used, (but not to the author's actual knowledge) ran as follows:

> Here is where poor Henry lies,
> Nobody weeps and nobody cries.
> Where he went and how he fares,
> Nobody knows, and nobody cares.

As I have said, Henry was well known for his poetry; so well, in fact, that his friends were always asking him to make rhymes on the spur of the moment.

One day he dropped into a tavern up near Lorraine, where he found a group of acquaintances whiling away an idle hour.

"Hello, Henry, how about making us up a rhyme?" one man greeted him.

Returned Henry, "I have no time, I have no tools, to make up rhymes for a pack of fools."

*   *   *   *   *   *

Many years ago Andy Blount ran an extensive logging operation in the Mad River region, his loggers being quartered in a large boarding camp which was run by a man and his wife who did the cooking, baking, and took general care of the place. One day Mr. Blount, who was making a periodic inspection of the operation, was approached by the lady of the combine, who had a grievance which she wished to express.

"Mr. Blount, you'll just have to do something about these men," she complained. "Some of them are eating two or three doughnuts for breakfast."

It was then that Mr. Blount displayed a bit of the dry humor for which he was noted.

"Well, just make the holes in the doughnuts a little bigger," he said, "and let them eat as many as they want."

A certain man who used to live in Sandy Creek once saw an acquaintance trudging along the street, carrying a sack of flour under his arm.

Turning to a bystander, he said, "Just look at the damn fool. Taking home flour to feed his kids, and I'll bet he ain't got a quart of likker in the house."

* * * * * *

Lew Bellrose used to have quite a sense of humor, which he liked to display by the use of a little gag that he worked many times, and always with highly humorous results.

Whenever he would hear an acquaintance mention the fact that a certain person was of exceptional height, he would come up with the remark, "Just like my brother. He was an awful tall man too."

After this remark had been patiently sandwiched into the conversation several times, someone was sure to ask, "Just how tall was your brother, Lew?"

Lew would then scratch his head and look kind of bewildered.

"Well, I can't rightly say," he would drawl. "He was either seven-foot-nine or nine-foot-seven . . . can't just remember which. Anyway, I know he was an awful tall man."

* * * * * *

On the bank of Little Sandy Creek, about half way between the Twin Villages, Sandy Creek and Lacona, there used to stand a large and flourishing planing mill and woodworking shop. This establishment employed quite a group of men, and for a long time it was the policy of the management to allow the workmen to take home clippings and scrap material, for use as kindling wood.

As is usually the case, certain individuals took undue advantage of this privilege, and soon the shop began

166

to miss quantities of workable material. After a while the management clamped down, and issued an order that no one was to take home anything without the express permission of the shop foreman. The penalty for disregarding this order was to be immediate discharge.

One of the workmen was a colored man by the name of Ebenezer, who lived only a short distance crosslots from the mill, on what is now Salisbury Street. Eb traveled to and from work by means of a brush-bordered path that led to his back door.

One evening he was on his way home with a small bundle of scrap material on his shoulder, in spite of the recent order, when who should step from a clump of bushes but the foreman.

"What have you got there, Eb?" he asked the colored man.

Now Eb was scared out of six month's growth, but he kept his wits about him just the same.

"Got where?" he queried blankly.

"There on your shoulder," pursued the foreman, hardly able to contain his mirth.

The colored man rolled his eyes toward the bundle, only then seemingly aware that there was anything there at all.

"Now what's dat?" he queried, a sickly grin on his face. "Who in this wor' you s'pose put dat dere?"

* * * * * *

Sometimes a remark which was remembered and snickered over for long years after, was the product of the lack of school learning, a condition very prevalent in the old days. Many would not have been uttered at all had the originator known better. A perfect example of this type of humor was displayed by a man by the name of George Sherman, a farmer from the Sandy Creek area.

167

A cattle dealer came to Sherman's farm one day, and his attention was attracted by a nice looking calf.

"I'll give you a dollar for that calf," he said to Sherman. The farmer shook his head.

"I wouldn't be likely to sell it to you for a dollar, when I've already turned down seventy-five cents." he said.

* * * * * *

Another witicism of this category is attributed to an erstwhile resident of the Boylston-Lorraine area by the name of Emil Schumaker. Of German origin, this man was very industrious and well liked by his neighbors, even though he was a "furriner" who could hardly speak English well enough to make himself understood.

One day someone asked him the ages of his wife and himself, and his answer was a classic which was repeated over and over.

"Well," said Schumaker, "Mine wife she is dirty, and I am dirty-two."

* * * * * *

Even though his command of English was very sketchy and inadequate, this man was exceedingly sensitive about his lack of education, and was never known to indicate in any way that he could not read and write with the best. In fact, he went to extremes at times to create an impression quite the opposite.

One day he went into the Cottrell Hotel in Greenboro, and picked up a newspaper that was lying on a table. Taking it to a chair near a window, he sat down and soon became apparently engrossed in the news. But Nett Clifford, who ran the hotel, noticed that he was holding the paper bottom side up as he "read."

"Any news in the paper today, Emil?" he asked innocently, greatly amused by the German's subterfuge.

168

"Yah," answered Emil. "Much news."

"Read me some of it," requested Mr. Clifford. "I can't read very much, myself."

This pleased Schumaker very much, but it also put him into a tight spot. He must keep up the pretense to save his face, he knew, but what might be contained in those printed pages he had not the slightest idea. However, on the front page was a picture of a large ship, in this case, of course, bottom side up, and this gave him an inkling.

"Big wreck on ocean," he 'read' slowly. "Ship tip over. Many peoples hurted . . . some maybe killed."

* * * * * *

Grover Joyner and Rossel Stone were a great pair of funsters who were always joking and carrying on when they were together. One day Rossel started to tell Grover something about a man whom they both knew, but somehow the name had escaped him and try as he would, he could not recall it.

"Why, you know who I mean," he said at last. "He owns that big farm down there just this side of Whatcha-Callit's Corners."

"Why sure," came back Grover. "You mean Old Man What's-His-Name."

"No, not him," objected Rossel. "He's been dead ten years."

* * * * * *

Joe Moullette was an old French-Canadian gentleman who used to live on a backwoods farm up near Osceola, in Lewis County. One time his name was drawn to serve on jury, and after a great deal of persuasion, the commissioner of jurors finally got him into the courthouse in Lowville. Here one of the clerks took over the task of getting him duly registered.

"Your name?" the clerk asked innocently, not realizing what he was in for.

"My name Joe Moullette," said Joe. "Always has been."

"Where do you live, Mr. Moullette?" asked the clerk.

"W'y, ever'body know where Joe Moullette live," asserted Joe.

"Yes, I know, but where is it?" insisted the clerk.

"Same place," said Joe. "I ain't move. Live there pret' near forty year, now."

"What I mean," persisted the clerk patiently, "how would I get to your place?"

"Well, I tell you," replied Joe. "You want visit Joe Moullette, by golly, you come right along. You just go to Osceola, turn right around and come back five-six mile. I live right there, by golly."

* * * * * *

At one time a man by the name of Hough ran a harness and shoe repair shop in Lacona, and at this same place of business he also sold boots and shoes, clothing, and a variety of other merchandise.

Being of a kind and sympathetic disposition, Mr. Hough allowed many people to run up rather large bills, some of which he found somewhat difficult to collect.

One day he happened to meet a man who owed him a large sum. but who had not mentioned the fact or been in to see him for a long time.

"Say, John," Mr. Hough accosted him, "I wish you'd come in and do something about that bill you owe me. You know, the debt will outlaw itself in seven years, and it's been almost that long already."

"Well, now," said John, "I certain' don't want that to happen. Don't intend to beat you out of it. Tell you what . . . I'll be in your place in a couple of days. I'll get

170

some more stuff and renew that debt for seven more years."

*　*　*　*　*　*

A certain farmer from up near Shadigee, in Orwell township, was one day engaged in repairing a lumber wagon. This was in keeping with the custom of the times, when every tiller of the soil was more or less of a mechanic and depended largely upon his own ingenuity to keep his equipment in running condition.

On this occasion he was being assisted by his son, a lad of fourteen, who in spite of his habitual show of ambition, was not overly noted for his mental abilities. Being busy at other things, he asked the boy to measure the damaged reach of the wagon, so that a new one could be fitted in its place.

The young man took a ruler and started to follow his father's orders, but some time passed and no report on the required measurement was forthcoming. Finally the man grew impatient of waiting.

"Did you measure that reach yet?" he called to the boy.

"Yes," answered the youth in a somewhat puzzled voice.

"Well, what did it measure?" demanded the father.

"Near's I can make out," answered the lad, "It's six feet an' four feet, an' twice the length of the hammer handle . . . an' just a little bit more."

*　*　*　*　*　*

Snow, of early arrival, great depth, and long endurance, for which the Tug Hill area is and always has been famous, has been the cause of many tall tales and comical comments. Here are a couple, picked up at random, which have stood the test of time.

During the great storm that swept the region in the

171

early winter of 1879, Judge Dewey. who was stranded in Richland, sent a telegram to his home in Lacona, only six miles away. The wire read: Storm still raging and snow ten feet deep. Seven engines and one hundred people are snowed in here. Will be home on first train. Have John plow the garden the first of May for sure.

* * * * * *

"Tink" Hadley, an old time resident of Sandy Creek, used to declare that the Boylston hills was the place to go if one liked snow. He related that on one trip through that locality, in the middle of July, he came upon a woman whom he knew diligently digging into a huge pile of snow. Naturally his curiosity was aroused, so he stopped to talk.

"What are you looking for, Lib?" he asked.

"Snow," she replied.

"Well, seems like you've got lots of it right there," said Tink. "What are you diggin' so deep for?"

"Now I don't want any of this new snow on top," replied the lady. "Want some of that four-year-old stuff buried down under there. Melt it up to do my washin'. Don't take near so much soft soap that way."

* * * * * *

Frank Pelo was an old French-Canadian settler who at one time lived in Boylston township, between Smartville and Greenboro. Mr. Pelo owned a small farm, from which he eked out a precarious living for himself and family, during the spring and summer months. But when fall rolled around, and the hunting and trapping seasons were at hand, the farm pretty much had to look out for itself, so far as he was concerned.

However, being an expert at both hunting and trapping, Mr. Pelo took his full share of deer and bear, and some of the choicest furs came from his traps. An amusing story was told regarding one of his trapping experiences.

It seems that he had set a large bear trap in a runway near the Beach Schoolhouse, and not wishing to catch a human in the trap, he had a large sign printed which he placed on a tree above the trap. The sign read: "Bear trap, keep away."

One of his acquaintances read the sign upon passing the spot, and the next time he saw Mr. Pelo he jokingly said, "Frank, you'll never catch a bear in that trap. Why, you've got a sign up over it telling the bear right where it is."

Mr. Pelo didn't take the matter as a joke. In all seriousness he replied,

"Well, by golly, that's the first I ever knowed that bears could read."

And it was noted that very soon after that. the trap, sign, and all were gone from the place.

* * * * * *

An amusing tale attributed to the Tug Hill plateau has also been told about other Adirondack logging regions, so it is rather difficult to determine just where it did originate. However, it contained such an element of dry humor that I repeat it here for the benefit of those who may not have heard it.

It concerned life in an old-time lumber camp, when the wages were small and the going was tough. Winter daylight was short, so work began long before dawn, and went on until after dark at night. As one oldtimer put it, "It was two suppers in one night and hurrah for the brush."

It is said that one lumberjack approached his boss and told him that, on the next Saturday night, he was quitting his job.

"What's the matter?" asked the boss. "Ain't we treated you good?"

"Treated me fine," said the man.

"Dissatisfied with the grub?"

"Grub is fine," admitted the man.

"Then what's your reason for quittin'?" asked the boss.

"Well, I'll tell you," said the jack. "When I come here you promised me steady work. Lately it's been gettin' so sometimes I have three-four hours in the middle of the night when I don't have anything to do but sleep."

FAUD YANTIS,
THE DEVIL'S OWN

In the lives of the residents of most of the old-time rural areas, superstitious belief in witchcraft, evil spells, and second-sight played an important part in everyday living. Folks believed that certain individuals possessed evil powers, usually bestowed by the Devil himself, which enabled them to accomplish unbelievable feats. Many are the wild tales, embellished by their passage from person to person and year to year. that flourished in the past century and spilled over into this. Most of them have vanished into the limbos of time; a few still remain to amuse a more cynical breed, to whom so-called miracles are every-day fare.

Classic examples of these are the tales that still existed at the start of this century concerning the doings of Faud Yantis. Many a time the author has sat in the lamp-lit kitchens or "sitting rooms" of his parents' or grandparents' homes and listened to accounts of the wondrous and spine-chilling accomplishments of this man, as recounted by the local story-tellers. Later on, the sprint upstairs to bed was accelerated by the imagined hot breath of the sorcerer scorching his heels at every step.

No two people ever used to quite agree on the origin, nationality, or range of activities of Faud Yantis. He seems to have been identified with not only the Tug Hill country, but the whole of northern New York State as well. From the name, one would deduce that he was of

175

Dutch ancestry, probably Palatine Dutch. No known records exist concerning his birth, death, or officially, his very existence. Maybe the tales that used to be told about him were old-wives tales, figments of the imagination, or just plain hog-wash. Be that as it may, this writer knows for certain that such tales did exist early in the century, and they should be preserved as part of the folk-lore of the area.

Not much was ever related concerning the early life or activities of Yantis. No doubt he led a very commonplace existence until the time that his supernatural powers catapulted him into the lime-light of notoriety. There was, however, an account of how he attained those powers. Each version of this varies from its predecessors in minor details, but the essentials of all remain about the same.

It seems that Yantis, although his needs and desires were comparatively simple, was never able to fill them completely and to his satisfaction. Looking about him he saw others prospering while he, himself, never seemed to get ahead. After giving the matter a great deal of careful thought he arrived at the conclusion that if he possessed some kind of supernatural powers, everything was bound to be alright. There was only one way that he could think of to obtain these powers: from the King of Sin and Darkness, Satan. The Devil himself.

Here the whole matter seemed likely to end against a blank wall, because Yantis did not have the slightest idea of how to contact the Devil. Although he knew definitely that Old Nick was carrying on his nefarious work all around him every day, how to actually bring himself into the awful presence remained a deep and dark mystery.

After much surreptitious questioning, somebody at

176

last hinted to him that for a price, a certain old hag who was supposed to be some kind of a witch, would reveal to him the ritual by which he could bring about an actual contact with the Devil. Although she lived miles away, Yantis decided that the irksome travel would be well worth the while if the desired result was obtained. So one spring evening, just as the bats were beginning to swoop through the air on their nightly gyrations, he presented himself at the decrepit dwelling-place of the lady in question.

"Yes," the hag assured him, displaying a toothless smile in answer to his request. She could, and would for a price, reveal to him how he could come into the awful presence of His Satanic Magesty. The stated consideration was named and changed hands, and she proceeded to detail for him the procedure that he must follow.

"First," she said, "You must find a black-berry bush that is rooted into the ground at both ends, so that it makes an unbroke loop. It's got to be black-berry, no other will do. Then, when the moon is at its full in October, at just midnight, you must crawl backwards three times through the loop; repeating each time the secret words that I will tell you. When this is done, the Devil will appear to you, and you can make your deal with him. But beware, sinner, for he is a hard bargainer."

It is said that in later years, Yantis made no bones about revealing how he came by his supernatural powers, especially when he was in his cups. But although several people tried to worm the secret from him. he never did reveal the magic words that were imparted to him on that fateful night, and they went with him to the grave.

With this knowledge in his power he felt that he was well on his way to fame and fortune. But the going was not so easy as he anticipated. To begin with, black-berry bushes rooted into the ground at both ends were very hard to find. Search as he might, the first October full moon came and went and still he had not discovered this very necessary adjunct to his plan.

But the following spring he began to think that his luck had changed, for he did in fact locate such a botanical wonder. Yantis did a jig of joy upon making the discovery, and then thought ruefully of the long months ahead before the next October full moon.

But his joy was short-lived, for one morning he visited his treasure to discover that during the night some creature, probably a rabbit, had gnawed entirely through the plant, and it was now two very ordinary, mangled stubs.

At this point Yantis was, very understandably, about ready to give up. It is said that he once confided to an acquaintance that the idea suddenly came to him that this was the Devil's way of testing him, to determine the genuineness of his purpose in seeking him out. Be that as it may, he certainly displayed a pertinacity that would have been very creditable in a man with a higher purpose, for he immediately set out on a search for a second confused black-berry bush.

This time the quest was much shorter and easier. By searching almost incessantly he had by August discovered the second plant with the potential magical qualities. And this time he took no chances. Working feverishly. he constructed a rabbit and rodent proof fence around the bush, and to further keep it safe until the approaching witching hour, he camped out at the spot to keep all marauders away.

And so it was that the night of the October full moon came at last on dragging feet. And Faud Yantis, his precious black-berry bush safe inside its impenetrable bar-

178

rier, faced his great adventure. It may be safely assumed that he was nervous and apprehensive as the magic moment of midnight approached, being as he was only human. The owls hooted dismally as the disk of the moon slipped above the surrounding forests; and in spite of the light, the bats flitted crazily and abundantly in the area.

At last the moon stood almost directly overhead, and Yantis's watch, which he hoped fervently wasn't slow, pointed to midnight. Quickly he slipped through the narrow opening he had made in the barrier—almost fearfully he scanned the black-berry bush with his eyes. It was safe!

Dropping to his knees, he hurriedly crawled backward through the loop, repeating the secret words as he went. Again he passed in a backward circle through the loop. Up to this point nothing out of the ordinary had happened, and Yantis' courage almost failed him. But he kept doggedly on, and hardly had the words passed his lips on the third trip through when everything changed.

Immediately there was a tremendous flash of fire that almost blinded poor Yantis, and set the surrounding underbrush to smoldering. But as his sight cleared he beheld a sight never before imagined in even his wildest dreams. There before him, hanging by his forked tail which was hooked over the branch of a tree, arms folded and little flames dancing over his entire body, swung the Devil.

Oh, it was an awsome sight alright; and just as you or I probably would, Yantis dropped to the earth, groveling in the fallen leaves and debris on the forest floor. After a moment the Devil uncoiled his tail and dropped lightly to the ground, where he stood with his arms still folded and a fearful scowl on his terrifying face.

"Well," he thundered in a terrible voice, "why have

179

you summoned me here, human? You'd better have a good reason," he added threatingly.

"Please, your grace," stammered Yantis, "I do have a good reason. I want to become a sorcerer and have supernatural powers, And I believe that you. and you alone, can help me."

"So you really believe that?" mused the Devil. "Very commendable, very good indeed. Well, you're right . . . I can help you. But not without something in return, of course. How dear a price are you prepared to pay?"

"What do you ask?" quavered Yantis.

"Your mortal soul to do with as I wish when you die," returned the Devil.

"Your price is high," objected Yantis.

"So are your wishes," said the Devil. "Well. make up your mind. Take it or leave it. I have lots of work to do tonight and can't have my time wasted."

With that he began to twirl his tail "round and round," and Yantis, fearing that he was about to disappear, hastened to agree to the terms, exorbitant though they might be. It is said that Yantis in later life confessed that he had a plan to cheat the Devil by committing suicide in his declining years, but this apparently was not to be.

"Well, that is good," roared his Satanic Magesty. "You now belong to me body and soul, and in return, the powers that you wish shall be yours. But mind you, never use them to do a good deed. If you do you will immediately lose them, but your soul will still be mine. Now go out and do your damndest. Make the world a worse place to live in."

So saying, the Devil gave a tremendous bound and disappeared above the tree-tops in a towering pillar of fire. Weak and trembling, Faud Yantis dragged himself home.

Mad River forest fire observation tower, one of tallest in state.

*Breaking new hauling road through
Tug Hill snow.*

An abandoned Ward King lumber-camp on Tug Hill.

Camp on Tug Hill with a thick blanket of winter snow. (L. Lansing photo)

Tug Hill snow. Picture used in Civil Engineering course at Queen's University, Toronto, Ontario, showing snowload on a roof. (L. Lansing photo)

Log loader after sitting through a Tug Hill winter. (L. Lansing photo)

Snow survey tube used for measuring snow, showing 70" of snow on ground and 27" water content. Winter of 1963. (L. Lansing photo)

The Blount Lumber Company,
Lacona, New York.

The Gould (now Georgia Pacific) paper mill at Lyons Falls, New York.

*Snow Ridge ski slopes located on the
eastern side of Tug Hill.*

*Snow Ridge building complex at foot
of slopes.*

From that day he began to perform numerous feats of magic that snowballed with the telling until he became a legend in the North Country. But always the feats that he performed had an overtone of evil. Apparently he had no hates in his life, and very few dislikes, otherwise his power might have been used to bring grievous harm to the subjects of his displeasure. This was not the case, for he actually harmed nobody. Instead, he always seemed activated by personal greed and a wish for self-gratification. Probably most of these exploits have been blown up out of all proportion to the reality, just how much no one can tell at this late date. One thing is certain, the changes have been all in the direction of gain instead of loss.

Many of these stories were related to the writer by his uncle Charlie Hooker, who claimed to have had a friendly acquaintance with the sorcerer. But then, Uncle Charlie claimed lots of things that weren't always conversant with known facts. However, he possessed an open and inquiring mind that was far ahead of his day and age in many respects, and he was always good to the writer. And so the writer, in the innocence of childhood, swallowed all his stories as gospel truth, and here sets forth the ones concerning Faud Yantis for what they are worth.

One of the much related tales concerns the time that Yantis, desiring fresh milk and butter and perhaps a little beef later on, stole a prized Jersey cow. It appears that the cow's owner suspected as soon as he missed her what had become of her, and immediately swore out a warrant for Yantis' arrest. Armed with the warrant, the town constable set out to locate Faud and, if possible, bring him to justice. Riding along a back country road in his buggy, he suddenly came face to face with the wanted man, walking placidly along leading the cow on a rope. Pulling his horse to a stop, the constable leaped out into the road and confronted the culprit.

"Halt," he cried menacingly. "Faud Yantis, I arrest you in the name of the law."

"What for?" queried Yantis mildly.

"For stealing that cow," said the constable. "You did steal her, didn't you?"

"Yes. I stole her, alright," Yantis readily admitted. "Well, Mr. Constable, I guess you've got me dead to rights."

"Guess maybe I have," agreed the constable. "Tie the cow to the buggy and get in here with me," he ordered. "This time you're going to jail."

"Well now, let's not be hasty," said Yantis mildly. "First I want to show you a trick that I don't show to many."

Reaching into his pocket he drew out a ball of twine which he tossed into the air, holding to one end of the string. Up and up it went until it disappeared above the trees that bordered the road. And then, so the constable solemnly swore, Yantis climbed right up that string and also disappeared, leaving the open-mouthed officer standing there in the dust of the road. What was more, he took the cow along with him, still leading her on the rope. And to prove that it was not all just a bad dream, there was a big, steaming cow-flop right in the middle of the road.

Faud Yantis was not seen in that locality for some time after that, and no one ever saw the cow again.

Now, that was the story that the constable told, and as he was the only witness, who was there to say whether or not it was true? Perhaps Yantis actually outwitted the officer and made his escape in a less spectacular if more realistic manner, and he merely capitalized on the sorcerer's reputation to cover up his own short-comings.

182

Anyway, it is the kind of material that legend is made of, and it seems to be a human trait to like to believe such tales.

Another favorite anecdote concerns the time when Faud was visiting a certain Tug Hill area village, and happened to feel the urge to enjoy a meal of hotel fare. Marching into the best hostelry in town, he blithely ordered a large meal of the best quality that the house afforded.

Now the proprietor, being well aware of Yantis' usual indigent condition, naturally wondered if he would be able to pay for it, so he approached the table where the man was sitting and asked him, point blank.

"Why now," said Yantis mildly (all tales of him seem to agree that he always spoke mildly, with no cursing or blasphemy), "I guess I can take care of that."

Grasping one of the buttons on the old brown coat that he wore, he wrenched it from its moorings and rubbed it vigorously on his sleeve. Then opening his hand he held out to the amazed inn-keeper a shiny, new five dollar gold piece.

Still hardly believing his senses, the flabbergasted landlord took the coin and dropped in onto the table top. It had a genuine ring, and it passed the bite-test with flying colors, so still shaking his head in wonderment, he took it to the cash drawer and returned with four dollars and fifty cents change, which he gave to the placidly feasting Yantis.

After having leisurely finished his meal, he lighted a fat cigar, which he paid for with some change from the gold piece, and strolled from the place like a millionaire — still with one button missing from the old brown coat.

Later in the day the hotel-keeper related the incident to an acquaintance who dropped by; but of course the gentleman was somewhat reluctant to believe such a tale, and made his disbelief known, much to the annoyance of the landlord.

"But I tell you I saw it with my own eyes," he insisted irritably, "and what's more, I've got the goldpiece right here to prove it."

Opening the cash-drawer, he reached confidently inside, and then a look of utter disbelief came over his face. Slowly withdrawing his hand he opened it, and there on his palm lay nothing but an old brown button.

Although somewhat chagrined, the inn-keeper later used to joke about the incident, and say that he was glad that it wasn't a ten- or twenty-dollar button that he had to give change for. But how does one explain incidents such as this? Hallucination? Hypnotism? In this day of advanced psychic phenomenon, who can tell, or positively doubt?

Still another oft-repeated tale concerned a certain well-to-do man who habitually sported a flashy gold watch and chain which was greatly admired by Faud Yantis. This watch was of a distinctive design, said to have been made to order for its owner, as also had been the beautiful chain and attached gold medallion which was set with a large, brilliant diamond.

Yantis had many times been heard to express a wish to own an outfit like it, but he always added as an afterthought that he supposed such a thing to be impossible, as it was the only one of its kind in existence. So it was quite natural that he was greatly perturbed when the rich man, after his death, was buried still wearing the cherished treasure.

Faud's protestations against this apparent waste of wealth were often heard but generally ignored until one day, only a week or two after the funeral, he was ob-

184

served to be wearing, with a great deal of pride, an identical watch, chain, and fob. Of course he was at once taken into custody for questioning by the local constable.

"Where did you get Mr. - - - -'s watch and chain?" asked the officer.

"Why, yesterday as I was walking along the road down near the cemetery, there it was hanging on a bush right beside the ditch," replied Faud guilelessly. And no amount of further questioning could make him change his story one little bit.

In those days, grave-robbing for the cadavers was very prevalent, and of course Yantis was immediately suspected of this crime. But a thorough examination of the grave and its surroundings convinced the local officials that nothing had been disturbed or changed, so they were forced to release their prisoner. The watch and chain they returned to him, dismissing the affair as a remarkable if unexplainable coincidence.

But it happened that the man's widow heard of the affair, and her doubt was not so easily satisfied as that of the local officials. She was not at all sure that her husband's body had not been removed from the grave and sold for a few dollars to some medical school for experimentation. To put her mind at ease, she implemented the necessary legal steps to have the grave and casket reopened before witnesses. When this was done, there were the man's earthly remains resting as peacefully as when he was buried — but without the beautiful watch, chain, and diamond fob! And a thorough search of the coffin failed to reveal any sign of them.

Of course Yantis was once more brought in for questioning, but this time the coveted jewelry was missing. When asked what had become of them, his only answer was, "Lost 'em." And as no one was able to prove differently, he was once again released to go his evil way.

Another time, Yantis was accused of stealing a horse and buggy in Glenfield, a saw-mill town on the Black River just off the eastern shoulder of Tug Hill. The owner of the rig swore that he saw Yantis drive away in it, and although he gave chase on foot, some invisible force prevented him from catching up, even though the thief appeared to take a very leisurely gait. At last fatigue forced him to give up the chase, and Yantis, horse, and buggy disappeared down the road.

Now the time of this happening was determined to be six o'clock in the evening, as the saw-mill gangs were just getting through work for the day. Several of these men also claimed that they saw Yantis driving the horse and buggy down the street. Yet when he was arrested for the theft, the sorcerer was able to produce half a dozen witnesses who saw and spoke to him in a general store in Richland, at about six o'clock on the very day in question. Assuming that both sets of witnesses believed themselves to be telling the gospel truth, the question of how the remarkable transfer was accomplished arises. Richland was and is at least thirty-five miles from Glenfield as the crow flies across the rocky crest of Tug Hill, and nearer sixty following the tortuous, rutty roads of the era. And of course there were no automobiles or airplanes in those days. So how did he manage to cover all that distance in just those few minutes?

However, and if, the feat was accomplished, be it deception or otherwise, the Devil was again on Yantis' side; the case was dismissed and the sorcerer won yet another tilt with the law.

The foregoing are only a few of the stories that once existed concerning the doings of this remarkable individual. The writer himself heard them related in his early childhood, and needless to say, they made an impression on his young mind that has remained virtually unchanged through the many intervening years. Today they remain bright and unfaded where many other more important matters have been forgotten. Ah, but to possess the other tales that once were told and breathlessly listened to, but which are now irretrievably lost and forgotten.

No one knows for sure just how old Faud Yantis was, or what was his age when death overtook him. But all accounts agreed that he was a very old and still very agile man when the Devil finally claimed his own. It seems that although he was capable of performing wonderful feats of magic, he was still susceptible to the infirmities of the human flesh, and "lung fever," or pneumonia, at least laid him low.

As he had no known relatives or anyone to care for him, the men in the neighborhood of the ramshackle residence that he called home at the time, took turns at sitting with him and giving him what care they could. Thus it was that an eye-witness was present at his passing.

This man later related that the very sick Yantis had lapsed into a sort of coma, from which no one expected him to emerge. But at exactly midnight on the last night of the death watch, a singular change took place.

Suddenly springing upright in his bed, the sick man uttered a terrified shriek and gesticulated wildly toward the door.

"There he is," he screamed. "He's come for me . . . make him leave me alone."

Somewhat alarmed, the watcher sprang from his

chair and looked around the room. No one was there, of course.

"There now, Faud," he tried to soothe the sick man. "Lay down and rest. There ain't no one here but me and you."

"Can't you see him?" shrieked Yantis desperately, pointing toward the doorway. "Hangin' there by his damned tail. He's come for me sure. The bargain we made . . . "

With a last rending scream, Faud Yantis, the magician, slumped down on the bed. Then a violent shudder and a rattling gurgle in his throat announced the fact that he was dead.

So did His Satanic Majesty claim his reward. For the lone watcher swore afterwards that the whole house stank of brimstone for an hour after.

TALES TALL, WILD, AND HANDSOME

Away back many years ago, conversation was a popular form of entertainment and the swapping of opinions and reminiscences was pretty likely to occur whenever and wherever two or more persons got together to spend a leisure hour.

At such times, somebody was almost certain to bridge the gulf between actuality and fancy by the telling of a tale which could not fail to tax the credulity of even the most gullible listener. Then for a time wild and improbable stories would fly thick and fast.

These tales usually concerned something which the narrator had either seen or done, and were told for amusement purposes only. Nobody was supposed to believe them and nobody actually did, not even the teller himself, even though he might relate them as though they were the gospel truth. No doubt they were a form of emotional escape, both for the teller and the listener, from lives that were oft-times very drab and uneventful.

However that may have been, they were always good listening, and amusing even when heard repeated and from different sources. Following is a selection of these tales which the writer has heard related in many places, ranging from lumber and hunting camps to his parents' own fireside when he was a small boy.

* * * * * *

"Talk about hard times," one old settler used to say.

189

"We really had it tough when I first come to Boylston as a young man and tried to grub a living from that little chunk of frost that was knowed as a farm.

"We used to have to grow or make most everything that we needed . . . couldn't afford to buy anything. Raised our own corn for johnny-bread and our buckwheat for pancakes. Et salt pork most of the time, 'cept for now and then when we could knock over a deer or snag a mess of trout. Made our soap from lye and bear grease. Even made the harness for my horses out of rawhide.

"Remember one time I was skiddin' logs with that rawhide harness. Had myself a mighty good team . . . they'd try to pull Tug Hill over if you hooked them to it. Well sir, I'd just fastened onto a big old butt log, scale a couple of thousand feet, anyway, when up comes a sudden shower. One o' them quick an' devilish kind you get in May, sometimes.

"Didn't figger on gettin' any wetter than necessary, so I yelled at the horses and away we went, hell-bent-for-'lection. Got to the skidway and started to unhitch, and by golly, there wa'nt no log there atall. All I could see was them rawhide tugs leadin' back through the woods. Of course the rain had soaked 'em up, and they certain sure had stretched out some.

"Well, I took the harnesses off and looped 'em over a big stump, an' went on to the barn. Pretty soon the rain stopped and I went back to the skidway, and by the time I got back there the sun had come out again. 'T wa'nt long before I looked down through the woods an' there come that danged log, amblin' along as pretty as you please. You see, the sun was dryin' them tugs out again, an' as they shrunk they dragged the log along in.

"That kinda set me to thinkin', and 'T wa'nt long

190

before I'd bought up all the rawhide I could find an' put it to skiddin' logs. Made myself a pile of money that summer."

*   *   *   *   *   *

Fred Guy, who for many years ran a restaurant in Lacona and was something of a sportsman in his younger days, used to tell a tale about an alleged experience which he once had.

"Was camped up near the head of Mad River," Fred would relate, "fishing the State Meadows for a few days. It was along in May and the trout should have been biting, but they weren't. Fished all afternoon of the first day and didn't catch even enough for my supper.

"While I was on my way back to camp I had to pass a swamp-hole that was alive with frogs, so I got myself a club and went frog hunting. In no time at all I had quite a heap, so I skinned out their hind legs and took then back to camp to cook for supper.

"Well, I washed them and put them in the frying pan and set them on the fire, and they began to kick and squirm as frog's legs will when they're cooking. Didn't think much about it, and turned around to get the coffee out of my pack-basket. When I turned back the frying pan had disappeared.

"That kind of mystified me for a minute, until I looked down towards that swamp-hole. There went those darned frog's legs, heading for home and taking my frying pan with them. It's a lucky thing I had a shotgun right handy, or I guess I'd never got that pan back."

*   *   *   *   *   *

"Snow . . . " said Sheridan (Sherd) Cross reminiscently. "You think we've got snow this winter? Well, let me tell you about the days when we really used to get snow.

191

"I remember one winter when I worked in the woods for Andy Blount, up above Plantz Corners. The snow come early that year and stayed late, and kept piling up most of the time between. The boys cut logs all winter, but when spring finally come they had to go back and cut another twelve-foot log off every stump.

"One day I was drivin' Andy's team of light road horses hitched to a cutter, taking him down a hauling road on an inspection trip. One of the horses threw a shoe, and as it was almost brand new, I didn't want to lose it and spent quite a little time looking for it. Couldn't find it though, so we drove on.

"One day the next July, I was passing that way again, and happened to think about that horseshoe . . . so I started looking for it. Pretty soon I saw it, hanging in the crotch of a little tree fourteen feet off the ground. The hauling road must have gone right over the top of it the winter before. So you think we've got snow, do you?"

* * * * * *

Fred Caster walked into the blacksmith shop in Redfield Square, and was greeted by a small group of acquaintances, who were lounging about in the cool shade. It was mid-July, and the weather outside was hot and sultry.

"Hot enough to suit you?" somebody asked Fred as he came inside.

"Why yes . . . sure is a corker, ain't it?" said Fred, wiping perspiration from his face with a red bandanna. "Never knowed it be hotter, except once. That time I lost the best team of horses I ever owned."

"Sunstroke?" asked one of the group, this appearing to be a reasonable deduction.

"Nope," answered Fred. "Frostbite."

192

This did not seem plausible at all, but the members of the group merely exchanged knowing glances and nobody made any comment. A story was coming, they knew.

"Happened in the fall of '92, or maybe it was '93," resumed Fred. "Come a Sunday in September when it really turned hot. Cooked the hen eggs right in the nest, and by golly, we dug potatoes that day that was already baked.

"Had a big field of pop-corn that was just about ready to harvest, and along in the afternoon it started to pop. Well sir, by supper time it had just about filled up that field, and was startin' to overflow into the horse pasture. Them fool horses of mine seen it an' lay down in it to cool off, thinkin' it was snow. And danged if they didn't lay right there and freeze to death."

*   *   *   *   *   *

"Strong? Well yes, I guess you might call me that," admitted Mart Thorpe modestly. "Fact is, when I was out West I was knowed as bein' right stout. Got the reputation in a funny way that I'll have to tell you about.

"Was helpin' a bunch of fellers raise a barn frame, out in the State of Michigan. Timbers was all hewed out of solid oak, green as could be an' heavier'n tunket. We had the main frame all up, an' was just startin' to raise the purline bent when somethin' slipped, an' everybody started jumpin' to get out of the way.

"I was standin' on a main beam sixteen-eighteen foot above the floor, when that hull danged purline bent started fallin' right down towards me. Knowed if I didn't ketch it, some of them fellers down below was goin' to git hurt real bad, so I just stopped it with my shoulder an' stood there holdin' it until the rest could git it propped

193

up with pike poles. By that time it was gittin' kind of heavy, an' I was glad to let go."

"How much do you think it weighed, Mart?" someone asked.

"Don't rightly know," said Mart. "But I do know that when I started to walk away, I couldn't move either foot. The weight of that bent had sunk my boots two inches into the solid oak, an' it took two men ten minutes to chop me loose. Always after that I was knowed as bein' quite husky."

* * * * * *

"Doctors," snorted Dan Butts. "I suppose they're alright in a way, far as they go. But there ain't one in a thousand that's got the real curin' touch, like my old grand-daddy used to have. That man could cure anything ever had by man, woman, or beast, even though he wasn't no doctor. Used to do it with herbs and things.

"I remember a salve he used to make out of boneset, spruce pitch, bear's oil, an' a few other things that he'd never tell about. Said it would cure any wound or sore that ever was, an' I guess it would. He never went anywhere without a little tin box of it in his pocket, an' it got to be famous all around the country.

"Took some with him when he went to war in '61, an' it certain come in handy one day in a battle. Feller right next to grand-daddy got his head cut slick an' clean off with a sabre slash, an' he just reached right down an' scooped up the head, slapped a little of his salve on it, an' set it back on where it belonged. In a couple of day's time the feller was alright again.

"Only thing wrong was that grandpa hurried a little too much an' got the head on backwards. Feller turned out to be a great scout after that, because the rebels couldn't never tell for sure which way he was lookin.'

194

"But after the war was over, he got to be a terrible thief. Nobody could ever catch him, because they always tracked him the wrong way. Couldn't nobody figure out that he was goin' in the opposite direction from what his tracks p'inted. Things turned out alright, though. After a while they made him sheriff an' he reformed."

* * * * * *

"Well now, you've heard tell of a man bein' restless as a fish out of water," said Charley Hooker. He had just filled and lighted his pipe, and now he leaned back in his chair and propped his feet on the stove-hearth. "But I guess they didn't mean the same breed of fish that I used to have for a pet. That one was more to home out of the water than he was in.

"Went fishin' one day when I was out West, in one of them muddy little cricks they have out there, an' caught myself a nice mess of catfish. Took 'em home an' put 'em in a tub, figurin' on dressin' 'em out for supper; but all at once one of 'em kinda caught my eye. Nice little feller about fourteen-sixteen inches long. Been outta water a couple of hours at least, but he seemed lively an' chipper as all get out.

"Put him in a pail of water by himself, an' he seemed so almighty thankful an' cheerful that I made up my mind to keep him for a few days. Longer I kept him the better I liked him. He got to be a reg'lar pet . . . would take worms an' things right outta my hand.

"Things got pretty dry that summer, an' water was awful scarce out West. Couldn't spare much for my catfish, so I started givin' him less an' less. Two-three weeks time I had him weaned away from water altogether. After that he'd foller me around all day like a dog. Got so he'd even come when I whistled to him.

"After a while I made up my mind to come back

195

THE PESTIFEROUS
BULL-FLY

Old-time lumberjacks were a rough, tough, and rugged lot, as they were always ready and anxious to agree, and even to demonstrate if the occasion demanded.

This was especially true of the French-Canadian breed of jacks that infiltrated the Tug Hill area from camps in the Adirondacks. An amusing tale concerning one of these was related many years ago to the author, by Francis Byrns, who as a young man spent many years as a lumberman and teamster in the Big Woods.

Mr. Byrns was guiding a sport from Syracuse cross-country to the headwaters of Millstream, where they intended to enjoy a day of trout fishing, when they came upon one of these Canuck woodsmen. This man was trimming out a trail to be followed by road-monkeys in the construction of a tote-road to a lumber camp. Of course, they stopped to chat with him.

It was mid-June and the black-fly and mosquito crop was at the heighth of its yearly cycle. All morning the two men had been tormented by swarms of the pests, and only liberal applications of oil-of-tar and citronella had prevented their being eaten alive. As they visited with the woodsman, they renewed the protective coating on their hands and faces from a bottle of this mixture, some of which they offered to him. This he refused, displaying an amused disdain.

"Franchman, she's no need fly-dope," he assured them. "Franchman, she's tough. If fly bite Franchman, she's get broken jaw, and teeth all fall out."

"Oh come now," scoffed the city sport. "I don't believe that you're really as tough as you make out you are."

At this the Canuck bristled visibly. "Franchman not lie," he growled. "W'en Franchman say she's tough . . . she's tough. Fly get taste of Franchman's sweat she's fall down dead on ground."

"Well, if you're so almighty hard as you say," countered the city man, "how'd you like to make ten dollars?"

Somewhat mollified, the woodsman agreed that he would, indeed, like to make ten dollars, and asked how it might be done.

"It's simple," said the sport, sensing a chance for a little fun. "You just drop your pants, hang your butt-end over that log, and let the flies chew you. If you can stand it for five minutes without brushing one away, the ten dollars is yours."

This seemed too good to be true to the Canuck, who desperately wanted that ten dollars, and he readily agreed. Sliding his suspenders from his shoulders, he let his stagged woolen trousers slide down until his bare buttocks were exposed, after which he calmly seated himself upon the log and let the insects begin their work.

The city man had taken his watch from his pocket to measure the allotted five minutes of time. This was one of the old hunting-type timepieces so popular in the old days, with a snap cover and a hinged crystal which swung out. This could be used for a sun-glass, and the remembrance sparked a devilish idea in his brain. Suddenly he decided that he was going to get full value for his money.

"This easy . . . too bad tak' your money," boasted the woodsman. The flies were chewing him unmercifully, but so far he had not flinched or paid them any outward attention.

Stepping unobtrusively around behind the man, the city man held the watch crystal in such a position that the sun's rays were focused through it. Gauging the distance carefully he drew the rays down to a sharp, burning point, which he centered on one of the exposed hips. As it touched him the woodsman gave an involuntary twitch, but did not utter a sound.

Not wishing to be overly cruel, and fully intending to fork over the money anyway, the sport withdrew the ray and centered it in another spot. This was repeated several times, to the increasing discomfiture of the man seated on the log.

The squirming increased, and soon he could stand it no longer.

"How much time left?" he inquired.

"One minute . . . if you can stand it, the money is yours," said the sport, trying to suppress his glee.

"Tell you w'at," countered the uncomfortable woodsman. "We mak' bargain. I tak' five dollar . . . you let me bat dat dam' big bull-fly w'at been foolin' around'."

THE MAN CALLED
HARDWOOD

His real name was Frank, but very few of the lumber-jacks, saw-mill men, teamsters, and farmers with whom he worked and associated knew or called him by that. To them, almost to a man, he was Hardwood — Hardwood Jones.

Probably the first reason for this peculiar monicker was his skill as a cutter, skidder, and roller of hardwood timber among the rugged hills of Boylston, Redfield, and Orwell townships. But later, when he left these pursuits to follow the slightly more gentle ones of farming and blacksmithing, the name stuck. To those who knew him, the reason for this was obvious. His whole makeup, bone, sinew, and nature, was hard wood through and through.

Farther south, in the hop-growing country of Madison County where he used to hire out as a picker each summer for many years, two other propensities of his were rather widely known. One of these was his liking for hard liquor; the other his skill and ferocity as a rough-and-tumble fighter. Of these facts many a hard-bitten old hop-picker at the turn of the century could bear testimony.

In at least one instance, the term "hard-bitten" was no exaggeration. The story goes that Hardwood, who was a smallish to medium-sized man, and a big bruiser from Chenango County were engaged in one of the almost nightly brawls with which the hop-camps were entertained. Hardwood had his man down flat on his back, and from his position astride the fellow's chest, was merrily pummeling every exposed portion of his head and face with fists hard as iron. In some way either by design or accident, one of his thumbs slipped into the mouth of the under-dog, who promptly clamped down on it with teeth large, sharp, and serviceable. Moreover, not content with biting, the man started to chew.

Now this was probably as ethical as most practices in the catch-as-catch-can fighting of those days, but it proved both distasteful and painful to Hardwood. Flail as he would with his free fist, he could not make the fellow let go. In spite of repeated threats of dire consequences, he still continued to chew like a dog-coon on a black-and-tan hound. Hardwood knew that if he was going to save even a bloody stub of that thumb he had to do something right away. So he did it.

"If that's the way you wanta fight, that's the way we'll fight," snarled Hardwood, and reaching swiftly down he grasped his opponent's ear firmly in his own teeth. Then with a mighty heave he reared back, shaking his head like a puppy tugging on a root. The ear came away suddenly, accompanied by an agonized yell from the Chenango bruiser, who, with all fight suddenly gone from him, began to frantically holler "Enough." However, this did not deter Hardwood from hitting him a few more smart raps, until he was pulled from the thoroughly beaten man by several bystanders.

"Didn't you hear him holler that he had enough?" asked one of the onlookers. Hardwood, busily wrapping his mangled thumb in a handkerchief, looked up with his one good eye twinkling.

"Certain, I heard him alright," he admitted, "but

he's such a damned liar you can't believe a word he says."

The writer's father, who was present at the time, has related this tale many times. He also said that some jokester with a rather grisly sense of humor, nailed the dismembered ear up to a post in front of the hop-house, where it remained until it dried up in the sun; an eloquent reminder to one and all not to tangle with Hardwood Jones. As to the one-time owner of the ear, he drew his pay that evening and disappeared. Hardwood carried the scars of the chewing on his thumb to his grave.

The writer's personal memory of Hardwood began some years after he had left the more rigorous occupations of his early life, to run a medium-sized farm at Castor Corners, near Orwell. Here he labored long, uncomplaining hours to help bring up several step-grandchildren who had been left parentless.

At this time he was a medium-sized individual of rather advanced age, tough and wiry as rawhide and seldom ailing a day of his life. His rather florid and craggy face was decorated by a bristling white moustache, and somewhat softened by the twinkling of one blue eye, its mate being blank and sightless from a mishap in early life. His head was bald and shiny, rimmed by a halo of wiry white hair, and habitually covered by a battered felt hat. This he wore jauntily askew over one ear, indoors and out, winter and summer, and from morning 'til night.

Visitors and neighbors were always welcome at the home of Hardwood and his wife, "Aunt Marthy," who was a notable character in her own right. Few who visited there were ever permitted to leave without partaking of at least a lunch, or even a full meal. It was a fav-

205

orite overnight stopping place for the pack-peddlers and
other itinerant wanderers of the rural areas. And no
neighbor with sickness or trouble in the family ever appealed in vain for help from the Jones's.

An amusing tale is told concerning Hardwood's liking for strong drink, be it whiskey, hard cider, or the
extremely potent clear grain alcohol so popular in those
days.

It seems that the men and boys in and around Orwell
had decided to form a fife and drum corps for the purpose of parading on the Fourth of July, Decoration Day,
and other momentous occasions. At that time, within
easy memory of the close of the Rebellion, patriotic fervor ran high and everybody and his brother wanted to
join. Among these was Hardwood, but in his case there
was one serious drawback. He could neither play any
instrument or beat a drum with any degree of rhythmic
satisfaction. Nothing daunted the other members, who
wanted him in the group because of the merriment that
they knew he would create, and they decided to let him
march at the head of the column and carry the flag.

Enthusiasm ran high . . . practice sessions were run
off with great asperity and success. At last came the
great day when the Orwell Fife and Drum Corps were
to march in their first Decoration Day parade.

It was just as the organization was about to form up
for the start that some well-meaning person made the
mistake of producing a couple of quarts of only slightly
diluted "alky," brought along for the purpose of streng-
thening morale and sharpening their step. In Hardwood's
case it did both, and something more; it made him a
little forgetful.

The group got away in a veritable blaze of music and
patriotism. Fifes shrilled and drums banged, each mem-

ber stepping high and precise. Right up front, walking on air and a noticeable aura of alcohol, marched Hardwood, really outdoing himself in precision of step and motion. It was not until the parade was half way to the cemetery that anyone noticed something was wrong.

"Hey, Hardwood, where's the flag?" someone in the crowd shouted.

Hardwood looked around in amazement. He had completely forgotten his purpose for being there, but he wasn't going to admit it.

"What flag?" he shouted back amid a road of merriment from the onlookers. "Well I'll be danged . . . I thought one o' you fellers had it."

After that, people say, he always made doubly sure he had the flag whenever the group started a parade.

THE MAD FIDDLER

Probably very few people in northern New York, in this present day and age, are familiar with the name Nicholas Goodall. Indeed, without a doubt, very few have ever heard it, or have given it more than passing notice at the most.

But a century ago conditions were different. Nick Goodall was well known then, not only in the North Country, where his fame as a musical genius reached its zenith, but also throughout the vast region that stretches between the Mohawk and St. Lawrence Rivers, and Lakes Ontario and Champlain.

Where he really came from has always been something of a mystery. But the fact that he ended his days in the Jefferson County alms-house, and now lies buried in the old cemetery on Arsenal Street in Watertown, are well documented certainties.

In the latter half of the past century he was known only as an eccentric fiddler, tramping the roads winter and summer with a black case containing his beloved violin clasped under his arm. Many times he walked or sat, even sometimes in the company of other people, with a vacant, far away half-smile on his face; as though he gazed upon scenes in a world all his own, inaccessible to any other but himself. At such times he might be heard to mutter strange words that had no meaning for any other brain than his.

209

But it was in the realm of music that his soul found its true expression. Through the magic strains that he produced by the expert strokes of bow over violin strings, his very being seemed to flow outward and upward, bathing his listeners in a warm sense of beauty and well-being, and spreading to the four horizons and the very heavens above.

And well it was for him that he did possess this talent for music, for he had no other skill or craft by which he could earn his precarious living. Never was he known to work, or to stay for long in any one place. His preference was to roam the highways and byways, ranging far and wide, stopping for the night wherever he could exchange fiddle music for food and lodging. And he was always welcome, whether in taverns and inns or in isolated farmhouses or lumber-camps, so starved were the people of those days for music and entertainment.

If he needed shoes, a pair could always be obtained from some cobbler in exchange for music. In the event that clothes were required, his violin, like the genie from Alladin's wonderful lamp, provided them for him. The fact that most of these garments were second-hand and too large for his rather delicate frame seemed to matter not at all. But the overall result was that he sometimes presented a rather ludicrous appearance as he trudged along the dusty or snowy highways.

It was said by some who claimed to know, that Nick was the son of a famous New York composer and orchestra leader. His entire boyhood was supposedly spent in almost constant enforced study and practice for a career in music. So great was the stress and strain of this rigorous routine that his mind snapped suddenly, leaving him little but his fabulous ability to extract heavenly melody from the strings of a violin.

His eccentricities were many and varied. Sometimes he could not be prevailed upon to play; at other times, once playing, he could not be persuaded to stop. It was said that many times he would sit in some inn or farmhouse for hours on end, utterly lost to the world in the music of the old masters. One by one his listeners would slip away to bed from weariness or necessity, at last leaving him fiddling away all by himself. Finally, as the sun rose over the eastern hills, he would rouse himself as from a dream, tuck his fiddle under his arm, and slowly trudge away down the road.

His musical talent was not confined entirely to the violin, but extended to the piano as well, and he was usually willing to play a few selections on this instrument whenever one was available. Legend has it that he could play a different melody with each hand at the same time, while he whistled a third.

Sometimes he would go for days with his hands swathed in bandages soaked in oil. When asked about this he would say that his hands hurt, but many times he would play even under this handicap, and people marveled at his ability to do so. It was said that nothing was ever actually known to be the matter with his hands which were marvelously soft and agile, probably kept that way by this unique method.

At times his appetite was that of a bird; at other times he would sit and gobble up everything placed before him as long as it was food, regardless of its nature.

At irregular intervals he could be prevailed upon to perform for pay at entertainments and socials, and one of these times produced a humorous situation recounted by Irving Bacheller in his book, "Eben Holden."

It seemed that an elder in a certain church one day came upon Nick standing beneath a tree and playing one sacred selection after another. After listening entranced for an hour, the elder persuaded him to perform that evening at a social gathering in his church, even though he knew full well that most of the congregation regarded the violin as a very instrument of the Devil.

The evening arrived, with a goodly crowd present at the church. During the preliminaries leading up to what was to be the main entertainment feature, Nick sat stolidly on a seat behind the altar, staring into space. At last the elder responsible for his presence there stood up to introduce him.

"Brothers and sisters," he announced, "we have the honor this evening to have with us a man whose musical talent surpasses any that I have ever known. Today I listened to him for an hour, and have persuaded him to come here this evening to entertain you with sacred music rendered on the violin. Friends, I would like to introduce Nicholas Goodall."

At the mention of the violin a murmur of disapproval ran through the crowd, silenced by a gesture of the minister's hand. Nick sat unmoving, as though he had not heard. Even when the elder approached and whispered in his ear, he made no motion or reply.

Somewhat embarrassed, the elder addressed himself to the congregation. "We shall first resign ourselves to social communion and the good things that the ladies have provided," he announced.

But hardly had the refreshments been brought out when the lone figure behind the pulpit suddenly aroused himself. Standing to his full heighth, he drew his bow across the violin strings, and the expectant hush was greeted by the lilting strains of "The Girl I Left Behind Me."

For a moment there was a stunned and horrified sil-

212

ence. Then a thoroughly affronted lady gasped, "Well, I never . . . " flung her frosted cake into a basket, and stalked from the church, head held high.

In a few minutes the general exodus had practically emptied the church. All that remained were the fiddler, who still played on and on, the elder, vainly trying to get him to stop, and a few of the younger generation whose greater curiosity and lesser fear of hell-fire and brimstone prompted them to stay and see what was going to happen.

At last the lilting melody ceased and the fiddler climbed wearily down from the pulpit. Slowly he made his way through the doorway into the bright moonlight of a balmy spring night. Slowly he passed between the gray granite slabs that cast their shadows across the green mounds of the churchyard. And then all of a sudden he again put bow to strings, and the night which had been silent was suddenly transformed into a thing of unutterable beauty.

Hour after hour he stood wielding the bow without pause or letup, wresting from the tortured and sobbing instrument the immortal melodies of Mendelssohn, of Brahms, of Handel, of Paganini. And hour after hour the few who had remained stood and listened entranced, unable to leave.

At last, just as the dawn was beginning to brighten the east, the lone figure seemed to come back to the world. Stepping along briskly now, he made his way among the tombstones to the highway. The works of the old masters was now replaced by the brighter and slowly diminishing strains of "Loch Lomond," swept back by the morning breeze as he made his way down the road and out of sight, "Oh you take the high road, and I'll take the low road . . . "

Only then did the small audience that had witnessed the impromptu performance manage to break the spell and make their way to their several homes.

Ole Bull, the famous Scandinavian violinist, was indirectly responsible for giving Nick Goodall his only chance at attaining international fame. Mr. Bull, visiting Elmira on a concert tour, heard of the eccentric musical genius and expressed a desire to meet him and hear him play. A meeting was arranged, and Nick was placed on the stage of a large auditorium in that city, while Mr. Bull sat far back in the empty theater, the better to take advantage of the accoustics of the place.

For a long time Goodall sat staring into empty space paying no attention to frantic signals to commence playing. At last Mr. Bull, tired of waiting, arose to go. He was half way to the door when the thrilling strains of the "Spring Song," rendered in a manner that he had never heard before, caused him to pause and turn back. Slowly he made his way to his seat, careful to not make a sound to disturb the mood that could produce such music. For three solid hours he sat there, listening breathlessly to an artist who played as though he had no idea that his audience was the most celebrated violinist of the day.

When he finally did leave because of necessity, Nick still sat there with head bent over his instrument, pouring out endless melody that made Mr. Bull shake his head in wonderment.

Later in the evening he remarked to a friend of his, a man by the name of John Nichols who was a dabbler in theatrical promotion, "That man is a real genius. He could be the greatest violinist in the world."

With this expert opinion in mind, Mr. Nichols went to see Nick and finally prevailed upon him to make a professional appearance under his promotion. Arrange-

214

ments were made for the use of a large theater in Troy, and on opening night the house was full.

In this, his only chance for fame, Nick Goodall ran true to form. As the curtain went up he sat unmoving, staring into space as though he were all alone in a world aeons away. After an unconscionable long time, during which the audience became understandably restless, he suddenly seemed to become aware of the violin and bow grasped in his hands. Tucking the instrument under his chin, he commenced to play.

Never had he performed better, and the audience settled down to breathless attention. Burst after burst of applause rose to the rafters, but with no apparent effect on the musician, who played tirelessly on and on. After two hours the manager wished to stop the music for an intermission, and signaled from the wings for a halt. But Nick only shook his head and played on. After a time the audience began to arise and leave, and soon the theater was empty except for stage hands and watchmen. Still there was no cessation to the music. The watchmen and stage hands dropped off to sleep, and still the music went on.

Just as the dawn was starting to break, the enraptured musician seemed to awake with a start, as from a deep sleep. Slowly and wearily he arose from his chair and made his way to the entrance of the building. Here he stood for a time looking out over the sleeping town. Then, placing his treasured violin and bow in their case, he tucked it under his arm and set out afoot on his trek back to his native habitat.

And that was Nick Goodall's one and only chance at real fame, a fame which apparently held no temptations and had no place in his patchwork existence of reality and fancy. For two more years he roamed the roads of the North Country, exchanging fiddle music for his meals and lodging, and tramping the highways in all kinds of weather.

One bitter cold morning he started out from a farmhouse near Hermon, in St. Lawrence County, with the temperature far below zero and neither overcoat on his back nor mittens on his hands. Some time later he was picked up half dead from exposure and frostbite, and althought he recovered, he was never again the same.

His lucid moments from that day on became farther and farther apart, and he became less and less able to provide for himself. At last there was nothing left for the authorities to do but place him in the Jefferson County alms-house, where he spent the remainder of his days, passing away in the late 1870's.

Thus passed a gentle and harmless soul, possessed of, or by, a great genius that might have brought him great fame and fortune under more propitious circumstances.

His violin, which was supposed to be of a very valuable make, was found upon examination by a group of experts to be only mildly valuable. It was purchased by a man from Evans Mills for the sum of $25.00, and the money was used to erect a marker over his grave in the Arsenal Street cemetery. This marker, like the genius that it commemorated, has since disappeared.

The violin, after passing through the hands of still another owner, was finally presented to author Irving Bacheller. It was believed to still be in his possession at the time of his death.

THE SNOW RIDGE
STORY

The severity of Tug Hill winters has always posed serious problems for the natives of the various communities affected by its numbing cold and raging blizzards. In the old days it was the deep and long-lasting snows that kept many families virtually isolated for days and weeks at a time. It was the far below-zero temperatures that made the chore of providing sufficient fuel to warm the homes a tedious and never-ending struggle. And it was the combination of the two that partly nullified the enjoyment and the benefits of living in an otherwise beautiful and beneficial land.

Later, since the necessity of keeping highways open and safe on a year-round basis has asserted itself, the same natural elements have played a prominent part in making life miserable for the men who are responsible for this gigantic task. Probably no where in the state do these dedicated men face more rugged conditions and overcome more obstacles, than on the highways that traverse the hills and valleys of the Tug Hill area.

These conditions are said to be caused by a thermal disturbance that has its conception in, and is peculiar to, the blunt eastern end of Lake Ontario. Here, winds that blow eastward across the lake pick up a tremendous load of moisture before sweeping inland and across the flat-lands of Jefferson and Oswego counties. As they encounter the upsweeping western face of the Tug Hill plateau, and follow upward over its crest, they deposit their moisture in the form of rainfall in summer and prodigious, blinding, smothering snowfalls in winter.

The average yearly snowfall in the area has been computed at two hundred and sixteen inches; and that, if it all fell at once, would amount to eighteen feet. Luckily, it does not all fall at once.

Is it any wonder, then, that one must marvel just a little at an enterprise that has taken these very elements that have plagued the region for years, and turned them to a purpose that has contributed immensely to the economic benefit of the surrounding countryside? Such is the unique winter-sports development known as Snow Ridge.

It all had its beginning away back in nineteen forty-five. After years of war-time austerity, gas and tire rationing, and conflict-weary nerves, all of which infringed sharply on the opportunities of Americans to have fun, the nation was emerging victorious but hungry and anxious for recreation and enjoyment. Never was there a more receptive climate for anything that promised people an opportunity to relax and unwind, and to a certain extent forget about the years just past.

Into this auspicious picture stepped two gentlemen who decided to do something about it. Lyman "Perry" Williams, a Boonville attorney, and Lawton Williams of Lyons Falls, no relation but a close friend and fellow ski enthusiast, took a long look around, recognized the favorable possibilities, and decided that a winter sports development was sorely needed in the area.

Accordingly, a partnership was formed and an organization known as Snow Ridge Ski Corporation was set up. With a working capital of $25,000, the two partners started a search for a suitable site for the development. A location near the little Lewis County village of Turin, named for the famous winter sports resort in Italy, was finally decided upon, land was purchased, and the work of clearing slopes was begun.

This locality, situated on the extreme eastern flank of Tug Hill plateau and overlooking the beautiful Black River valley, is one of the most picturesque in the whole of upper New York State. Its long, sweeping slopes and unfailing supply of bountiful winter snows, plus its easy accessibility from any one of several populous areas, promised perfect conditions for such a venture. And so they proved to be.

An internationally famous ski authority, H. Smith Johannsen, was engaged by the partners to make a survey of the site and lay out the basic ski trails. Two rope ski-tows, one of them at that time the longest in the state, were installed at strategic points. A farmhouse situated at the base of the slope was converted into a chalet with cafeteria, first aid and rest rooms, and a ski shop. By the time the first snows of the 1945-'46 winter season arrived, the development was operational and raring to go.

Peter Gabriel had been engaged as the head instructor of the ski instruction center connected with the enterprise. Mr. Gabriel, a native of Switzerland, came to the area well qualified for the position. Before leaving his native land he had served for twelve years as instructor on the famous St. Moritz slopes, after which he also instructed the Swiss Mountain Troops in advanced skiing. After reaching the United States he had served as a mountain guide on two important mountaineering expeditions, and from 1942 to 1945 as head ski instructor in the U.S. Mountain Troops. Truly, the two partners spared neither trouble or expense to secure top-notch instruction for their prospective clients.

The official opening took place during the 1945 Christmas holidays. As is usually the case, the first few weeks were a little slow. The place had to "catch on," to be accepted. First patrons were confined largely to local ski enthusiasts, but quickly the word spread that here in the Tug Hill country of upstate New York were to be found conditions and facilities unsurpassed by even the famous winter sports resorts of the New England states, Canada, and even Europe.

At first the turnover was five thousand skier-days per year. But gradually the field of interest widened, and by the time the 1946-'47 snow season rolled around, favorable word had spread to far distant places. Ardent ski fans and snow lovers began arriving from all parts of the state; from the New England haunts of the winter sports clan; from remote spots in Canada.

With success looking their way, the founders of the enterprise did not pause to rest upon their laurels. With eyes always to the future, they continued to expand and improve; adding new slopes, new and improved ski-lifts, more and better services and conveniences for their patrons. In 1954 the position of head ski instructor was taken over by Rudi Kuersteiner, another Swiss native, who, with a staff of able assistants, continued to furnish superlative instruction to all who desired it, from neophytes to experts.

And this struggle toward perfection more than paid off. By 1966, when the enterprise had reached its twentieth birthday, the scope of Snow Ridge had increased twenty-fold. Instead of the meager beginnings there were now nine well developed slopes ranging from begin-

220

ners' to expert, two fast racing trails, and a touring trail for folks who just wanted to take their time.

At the bottom of one of the original competition slopes known as The Rattler, an optional trail led over a 38 degree "schuss" referred to as the "Hu-da-thunkit." This trail was used only by very advanced or very venturesome skiers, as it was about equivalent to having the earth fall right out from under one's feet.

The two original rope tows had been replaced by three double-chair lifts and two T-bar lifts, capable of handling hundreds of skiers per hour. The facilities for satisfying hungry appetites whetted by the bracing winter air had increased to four cafeterias and snack bars. And at the quarter-century mark, the logging of one hundred thousand skier-days per season has become quite commonplace.

Snow Ridge has produced its full share of noted skiers. Notable among these were Miss Renie Cox of Port Leyden, a member of the 1960 Olympic team; Rick Lounsbury, 1965 national junior downhill champion; and Ken Phelps, a member of the U.S. Alpine team. And many bright lights in the skiing world have visited its slopes during the past twenty-five years.

Nor have the originators of the development gone without their share of honors and recognition as pioneers in their field. "Perry" Williams helped organize the New York State Winter Sports Council in 1947, and served for several years as its president. In 1970, Mr. Williams attended a meeting of the legal committee of Federation Internationale Ski, world governing body for skiing, held at Paris, France. Mr. Williams bears the distinction of being the only American ever appointed to this select group.

Truly, Snow Ridge has mushroomed from a mere

idea in the minds of two dedicated skiers, to become a unique and very important part of the economic life of Tug Hill country. Not only is this true of the institution itself, but also of the tremendous amounts of added income derived by the numerous ski-shops, restaurants, and motels that have burgeoned in the area.

And never once during all these years has Tug Hill failed to keep its promise of ever-abundant snowfalls and cold, sparkling weather. Verily, at Snow Ridge they love to see it snow.

AFTERMATH

On Sunday afternoon, August fifth, nineteen hundred fifty-six, there occurred in the little corner park, in the village of Osceola, Lewis County, an event which graphically illustrates the fact that, although most of the old-time woodsmen are long departed, their spirit still lives on in a few rugged individuals.

It was at this time that Percy Caster, the much younger brother of "Billy Ward" Caster, but himself a man well along in his second half-century of life, proved before a large crowd of onlookers that he could, as he had claimed, set a fullsized bear-trap without the use of either clamps, levers, or other mechanical devices.

Events leading up to the occasion had their beginning some weeks before at Pete Reid's diner in the village of Lacona, Percy's home town. Somehow an argument had developed among a group of local sportsmen concerning the use of old-time bear traps, and, as Mr. Caster was conceded to be the only local authority on the subject, the issue was left up to him to settle.

In the general discussion that followed, Percy happened to venture the opinion that the setting of these large and cumbersome devices, with their powerful springs, was a comparatively simple and safe matter for a man who understood his business. In fact, he declared, he had set many of them with his bare hands, without the use of either levers, clamps, or any other mechanical assistance.

223

Now Percy is not a large man, or a powerful appearing man, and immediately some Doubting Thomas offered to bet him ten dollars that he couldn't back up his boast by actually accomplishing the feat. The challenge was immediately accepted, and an invitation extended to anyone else who might entertain similar doubts to back up said doubts in a like manner. Right away Percy had a plethora of bets on his hands, all of which he proceeded to cover, large and small.

The question now arose as to where a bear trap might be obtained for use in the test. The use of these devices, once so common fifty to seventy-five years ago, has been outlawed for many years by the Conservation Department, and they have become almost as extinct as the dodo and the dinosaur. Only a few have been preserved as mementos of a vanished era, and these are exceedingly few and far between.

At last someone remembered that two of these rarities had been hanging for many years in the bar-room of The Salmon River Inn at Osceola, a little village nestled in a valley on the flank of Tug Hill. Within a few days, permission to use one of the traps in the test had been sought, and granted by Jim Finley, who owned both the hotel and the traps.

It must be understood that up to this time Percy had not seen the instrument that was to test his strength and ingenuity. Having used such devices for many years of his young life, he knew full well the wide disparity of their size and strength. And he entertained no doubts that his opponents would select the largest and strongest. But still he showed no outward signs of worry, so great was his confidence in his own ability.

This confidence did not hold true among Percy's friends and acquaintances. As interest in the forthcoming contest soared, controversy and discussion became rife and spirited. Some predicted he could do it, but many others were just as sure he would fail. Wagers on the outcome were freely offered and as freely accepted.

And interest in the affair was by no means strictly local. A lady reporter for a large Syracuse daily gave it a great deal of advance publicity in her paper, and the unusual aspect of the whole thing somehow captured public interest to a surprising degree. Conservation officials from Watertown planned to attend. Inquiries regarding the time and place of the contest were received from far and wide by the residents of Osceola.

The author had known Percy very well for many years, but knowing also the savage strength of a bear trap's powerful springs, he was numbered among the Doubting Thomases. A few days before the event was to take place, I met Percy in Wheeler's drug store in Lacona.

"Perce," I said, "I'm afraid you won't be able to do it."

"Well," returned Percy, "maybe you'd like a little bet, too."

"No thanks, Perce," I hastened to reply. "I know you too darned well for that."

The agreed-on Sunday finally arrived, and Osceola really came alive. Whereas, (as a news commentator put it) "Usually the only things buzzing on a Sunday afternoon are a few flies," the village on this Sunday was lined with cars and crowded with people. Many came out of idle curiosity; a few had a genuine interest. Very few had ever before seen a bear trap, or knew anything about setting one. A good natured, slightly Roman-holiday atmosphere prevailed. Nearly everyone understood vaguely that a human being was to face a test that would

225

either vindicate a boast or place him to roast on the griddle of public ridicule.

If Percy sensed any of this undercurrent, he certainly gave no sign that it worried him. At precisely two o'clock he strolled out to the little village park, closely followed by Bob Soule, a sort of unofficial chairman for the doubters, carrying the largest and fiercest of the two traps from the hotel.

This instrument, a large Newhouse fully two and a half feet long and weighing nearly forty pounds, was placed on the ground. And there facing it, weighing only 148 pounds, stood Percy, equipped only with his bare hands, a corncob pipe . . . and a twenty-penny nail.

He wasted very little time. First he knocked the ashes from his pipe and put it in his pocket. Then reaching down he grasped the jaws of the trap in both hands, placed one foot on the spring, and using back and arm muscles, forced the spring easily down until the nail could be inserted over it and beneath the lugs on the ends of the jaws. This held one spring in a compressed position while its mate was forced down in a like manner, the spiked jaws spread, and the pan and trigger adjusted. After that the nail was removed, and the trap became a deadly thing. As easy as that.

Some thoughtful person had brought along an old boot, and this was thrown into the trap to see if it really worked. It did . . . so effectively that it took four or five strong men to remove the boot from its spiked grasp.

"Gawd," someone in the crowd gasped. "What that thing would do to a hand."

Well, Percy collected his bets, quite a bit of glory, and, last but not least, a great big kiss from the lady reporter, who was of course present.

A good time was had by all, even the doubters who

226

had to pay up. There was a good deal of joking and good-natured raillery. But the really important aspect of the affair, noted by a very few of the more thoughtful and perceptive, was the proof that good, old-time self-reliance and ingenuity still lives on in a few rugged individuals in Tug Hill Country.